W9-BDL-743

To my mother

Promises I Made My Mother

Promises I Made My Mother

SAM HASKELL

with DAVID RENSIN

Foreword by
RAY ROMANO

BALLANTINE BOOKS · NEW YORK

Published in the United States by Ballantine Books,
an imprint of The Random House Publishing Group,
a division of Random House, Inc., New York.

BALLANTINE and colophon are registered
trademarks of Random House, Inc.

LIBRARY OF CONGRESS CATALOGING-IN-PUBLICATION DATA

Haskell, Sam.
  Promises I made my mother / Sam Haskell with
David Rensin; foreword by Ray Romano.
      p. cm.
    ISBN 978-0-345-50655-9 (hardcover: alk. paper)
    1. Haskell, Sam, 1955–   2. Theatrical agents—United States—
Biography.   3. Executives—United States—Biography.
1. Rensin, David.   II. Title.
  PN2287.H37A3 2009
  384.55'4092—dc22
  [B]   2009002856

Printed in the United States of America on acid-free paper

www.ballantinebooks.com

9 8 7 6 5 4 3 2 1

FIRST EDITION

Book design by Casey Hampton

For Sam and Mary Lane, Shirley,
Aunt Betty, Mary, and,
of course, Momma

Contents

by Ray Romano

When I met Sam Haskell for the first time, I was a little wary. It was at the beginning of *Everybody Loves Raymond* and until then I had never really dealt in great detail with an agent before. I had lived my whole life in Queens, New York, and, like most people, my perception of an agent was a fast-talking, slick, wheeler and dealer. I met Sam and it was a little different.

It was Gomer Pyle in a suit.

I really didn't know what to make of Sam at that first meeting. Here was this soft-spoken Southern guy who seemed polite, friendly, and genuine enough. Then I remembered my favorite *Twilight Zone* episode in which the Martians come to Earth and they're just that—polite and friendly—and after they help the humans with everything they need on Earth, they persuade them to come to their planet where everything is perfect. It's utopia. Of course as the humans board the ship, we find out that the Martians want them because there's a food shortage on their planet. They want to eat them!

I wasn't gonna let that happen. Sam Haskell was not going to eat me.

Okay, that sounds a little weird but I'm gonna leave it, because it was sort of the way I felt about that whole situation I was in. I wasn't gonna let the thrill of fame and success make me compromise my own morals. I feel I have a strong sense of right and wrong, and I think I owe that to my two brothers.

My brothers and I lived our whole lives in New York City, and while my path took me to stand-up comedy and ultimately Hollywood, they followed their hearts into two completely different careers.

My younger brother, Robert, worked at TNT in public relations, making a pretty good salary, and then at thirty-eight he quit to become a second-grade public school teacher in the Bronx. My older brother, Rich, served twenty years as a sergeant on the New York police force, ten of those in undercover narcotics. I know Robert loves working with underprivileged kids, even though it can be a thankless job, and I know Richard never compromised his morals, no matter what the situation was as a police officer.

I've never said anything really nice about them to their face 'cause we're brothers, and the sibling rivalry runs deep, but when I think of them I have to admit, they are my heroes.

Wow, that wasn't easy.

They're gonna give me a lot of crap when they read this, but that's okay.

It's true.

So with the *Twilight Zone* episode as a cautionary tale, and my brothers as my moral barometer, I made a promise to myself when I left Queens that no one in Hollywood, including this agent Sam Haskell, was going to eat me.

Still weird.

As time went on, I got to see more and more of Sam. Every new contract I had to sign, or negotiation we had, he was there. I would always be a little obsessive and start questioning the fairness of every deal. Of course I wanted what was fair for me, but I would also question what was fair for the other guy. While it was enough to drive some agents and lawyers crazy, I never once saw Sam waver or flinch. Maybe this guy is someone who might understand where I was coming from.

Maybe.

After a year or so, I got more confused watching Sam. Was he for real? Could a guy in this business get as far as he did being fair and honest? I know my brother did it in the police force, dealing with thieves and drug addicts, but this was different. This was *show* business. It's far more corrupt.

About the third year of *Everybody Loves Raymond* there was somewhat of a turning point for Sam and me. We filmed the show every Thursday in front of a live audience. Managers and agents, family and friends would always be milling around. I would always bring one of my four kids. One night, I was filming a scene where we had to stop for some technical reason for a few minutes, so I ran quickly up to my dressing room to use the bathroom.

When I walked in, there was Sam Haskell, the worldwide head of television at William Morris, on his knees, helping my twelve-year-old daughter with her history homework. I looked at my wife, who was sitting on the couch. She just shrugged her shoulders and smiled. It was that night that I thought this guy might be different. I mean, don't get me wrong, even with all the cutthroat and backstabbing in this business, I know there are good people here, real people, but c'mon, sixth-grade history!

Although I wasn't totally sure what Sam's deal was, I saw a man who maybe, just maybe, was what he appeared to be.

The next few years on *Raymond* were very interesting. At one point, Sam was negotiating my salary with the network, which would have given me more money in one week than my brothers make in one year. It was a weird place for me to be, and through all my guilt and neurotic emotions, Sam was there with his calm, wholesome demeanor—that Southern Opie charm that somehow made it all seem okay. Of course, the more money I made, the more he and his agency made, and that was always something I kept in the back of my mind, even while I was constantly impressed at how he pulled it all off with such grace and dignity.

However, it wasn't until I was in Amory, Mississippi, that I gave in to my instinct that this "agent" Sam was not one of those *Twilight Zone* Martians. Every two years Sam Haskell puts together a charity show called "Stars Over Mississippi." It takes place in his hometown of Amory, and it provides college scholarships for kids who can't afford to go but who excel academically. Sam had asked Doris Roberts and me to perform along with Whoopi Goldberg, Brooks and Dunn, Kathie Lee Gifford, and a whole slew of stars that he brought to Mississippi.

The first day there, Doris and I were part of the traditional "Stars Over Mississippi" parade that drove down Main Street in Amory. When I saw that Main Street was three blocks long and it had a store where you could buy slingshots, I realized this town was not a metropolis. But there I was, sitting in a convertible with Sam at my side, waving to all the Amory people who had come out to support what he was doing. They all knew about Sam Haskell, hometown kid, who had gone to Hollywood and made it big. You could see it in their faces, thinking, *He's back. Sam's back doing what he does. He brings Hollywood to us and he puts our kids through college. He didn't forget us.*

The show was the next night on a big outdoor stage with about ten thousand people in attendance. It was fun to do and the crowd was amazing. At the end, when we all came out on stage and took our bows, there was a feeling of accomplishment from all the performers and the people working behind the scenes.

It was a great thing to be a part of.

But there was something more that I noticed on that trip, which confirmed how I felt about Sam Haskell. To explain it, I need to tell you a quick story not about Sam, but about my identical twins, Matt and Greg.

When they were seven years old, I took them to see *The Lion King* in New York. They had seen the movie and were dying to see the play, not having any clue as to how it would look as a Broadway production. We got our tickets the last minute and our seats happened to be right on the aisle, but mine was one row behind theirs.

The music began, the curtain went up, and there was a character dancing onstage. While my twins' eyes were transfixed on the stage, I could see that from the back of the theater the whole cast of animal characters were slowly dancing to the music as they walked down the aisle. I'm talking huge giraffes, rhinos, and lions—all the animals in the play—and leading the way were the elephants. I think there were four actors, one for each leg, inside one of the ten-foot-tall puppet elephants that was lumbering down the aisle, as the song "Circle of Life" filled the theater. As they were reaching our seats, my twins were still facing the stage, not realizing what was behind them.

I watched to see their reaction as they turned their heads and got the first glimpse of this larger-than-life elephant dancing slowly down the aisle, and (I'm gonna get a little corny here) I saw what joy looks like. I'm not gonna try to describe it, or get too schmaltzy with it. Let me just say that I've seen my kids happy, having fun, laughing, and smiling endless times, and it still isn't the same as that one moment.

I will never forget that look.

Now, although it wasn't exactly the same and it came in different forms, I swear to you, during those two days in Mississippi, Sam Haskell looked like he had just seen *The Lion King* elephant. That's when I knew he was for real. You can't fake that look.

Don't get me wrong, Sam Haskell loved being a big-shot agent and we've been together for a lot of successful moments. However, up until then I had never seen the look in his eyes that he had during those two days.

When I came back from Amory, I told my wife what I had found out.

Sam Haskell wasn't gonna eat me.

Since then we've become closer and I've seen more of what Sam is all about. He took me back to Mississippi a few years later to help raise money for the Katrina victims and there was that look again: he saw the elephant.

People find it hard to believe that a guy with his outlook and approach to life can ever make it in this business, and that's what amazes me. He did and he still does, and I don't see him ever compromising who he is.

When he asked me to write the Foreword to his book I was honored. After reading it and learning more about his life—what inspires him, the things he's accomplished, the way he did it, and the core of who he really is—I felt I needed to call my brothers and tell them something.

My list of heroes has changed.

I have three now.

And the Cheer Man Came

First and foremost, have faith in your dreams.

—MARY KIRKPATRICK HASKELL

Even as a little boy being raised in rural Mississippi, I loved television. Back then, there were only three networks: CBS, NBC, and ABC—and in my hometown of Amory, Mississippi, we didn't even get ABC until the late sixties. Amory was founded in 1887 as Mississippi's first planned community, a town used as the halfway depot for the Frisco Railroad between Memphis and Birmingham. By 1900, the population was about seven thousand people, and it's never changed. I often compare it to Andy Griffith's Mayberry.

In 1964, when I was nine years old, *Bonanza* came on at 8 P.M. on Sunday nights. It was the number one show on television, my absolute favorite, and I watched it every week. That same year, *Hello, Dolly!* and Carol Channing won Tony Awards, *My Fair Lady* walked away with the Oscar for Best Picture, *The Girl from*

Ipanema won the Grammy for Record of the Year, The Beatles were named Best New Musical Artists, and Donna Axum was crowned Miss America. I had a major crush on Julie Andrews, who won the Academy Award for playing Mary Poppins that year. I knew all of this and more. I was a walking statistician of entertainment industry facts, and I shared them with anyone who would listen. I read *TV Guide* every week, as well as *Photoplay* magazine, to get the latest information about the world of entertainment and Hollywood, where I dreamed of working one day.

I also paid attention to the commercials, and one in particular because they aired it during all my favorite shows: Procter & Gamble's ad for one of its biggest products, Cheer laundry detergent. More than just proclaiming the detergent's amazing cleansing power (quite dull for a nine-year-old), the ad featured a wonderful-looking character called "the Cheer Man" walking through a neighborhood, ringing doorbells. He wore a big hat with the swirling Cheer logo. His uniform was yellow and blue with orange stripes. When a housewife answered her door, he would ask, "Do you use Cheer?" Her face always lit up in a smile. "Well, *yes I do,*" she'd say, and show him her box of Cheer. He'd smile and give her a check for ten dollars!

At the end, the announcer would say, "The Cheer Man is coming to your town."

The commercial promised that if he knocked on your door, and you could show him a box of Cheer or what they called "a reasonable facsimile" (basically, "Cheer" written on a piece of paper), he would give you ten dollars, which was an incredible amount of money for a kid in 1964.

The first time I saw that commercial I was not only absolutely convinced that the Cheer Man would come to Mississippi, but I was positive that he would come to Amory, and more important, to 405 South Third Street.

My home.

When I told my mother that the Cheer Man was coming, she never once pointed out how impossible that would be, or how far we lived from the places where those commercials were made. Instead, she told me it was a beautiful dream, and she helped me prepare for his arrival. Her support made me even more confident.

———

My mother used Cheer, but I wasn't content just to have the actual box or the word "Cheer" written on a scrap of paper when the Cheer Man came. No. Instead, I went to the local print shop with my fifty cents in weekly allowance, plus some money from running errands, and bought colored paints, glitter, and these "designer rocks" that people used to give texture to their artwork by gluing them on the paper and painting over them. I think my mother must have given me some money too, because it cost several dollars.

One Saturday afternoon, I made a giant sign with the Cheer logo, maybe three feet by four feet, and hung it on my bedroom wall. Then I waited.

Meanwhile, word of what I'd done spread across Amory, no doubt because I'd told the kids at school, and anyone else who would listen, that the Cheer Man was coming to my house. I'm sure most of them thought I was nuts. Still, I didn't care—my mother encouraged me to be a dreamer, and I believed anything was possible.

My insistence that the Cheer Man would come to our house soon became the joke of all jokes to my dad and his golfing buddies. When my parents had people over for cocktails or dinner, my father, Sam, Jr.—my grandfather was Sam, Sr., and I was Sammy—would say, "Sammy, go bring out your Cheer sign." I did, even though I knew how patronizing the laughter was. But I would look them straight in the eye and with every ounce of confidence I had, I would simply say, "He's coming."

My dad was a charismatic, handsome, self-made man who everyone wanted as a friend. He was close to the high school football and basketball coaches, and often hosted a gaggle of men at the house, where they'd drink beer and watch sports on TV. Although I know he loved us, my father was not a nurturer. His way of motivating his sons—me and my younger brothers, Jamie and Billy—was to call attention to our frailties. Though he would do it in a lighthearted, funny way, I never liked it.

My mother reacted differently. She believed in me and in whatever I believed in. She had taught me to always have faith in myself, no matter what. At the time I was too young for her to explain the reasons why faith couldn't hurt, only help—and I didn't ask deep questions—so it was her strong example that I took to heart.

When my father snorted in disbelief at what he thought was my fanciful imagination, she would say, "If he believes the Cheer Man's coming, then *of course* he's coming."

———

Time marched on. The commercial cycled off the air. I moved the sign from my bedroom wall to underneath the bed, and then I rolled it up at the bottom of my closet. But I still believed that somehow, someway, the Cheer Man would come to Amory—and more important, to my house.

The next summer, when I was ten, Jamie was having his ninth birthday party on Labor Day weekend. On any of our birthdays, there were always kids throwing a ball in the yard or playing a game in the quiet street. We had the run of the neighborhood, and as soon as we got home from school, we'd all be outside, doing things all over the place. Back then parents never had to worry about where their children were; today's dangers didn't seem to lurk around every corner.

At Jamie's party, we were playing football on the front lawn when suddenly we heard, from down the street, what sounded like a megaphone. Soon, we could make out the words: "CHEER! CHEER! CHEER . . . IS HERE!" Everyone stopped playing and stared. Then, in the distance, we saw a funny-looking car with a loudspeaker on the roof, driving slowly down Third Street like the Pied Piper of Hamlin on wheels, followed by all the kids in the neighborhood.

Oh my God, I thought. He's here! It's the Cheer Man! And it was true. The car was a few blocks away, but I was absolutely certain it wouldn't stop until it got in front of my house. I didn't waste a second. I ran inside to get my sign. All the other kids, who knew the story, followed me. Everyone grabbed for my mother's Cheer box, and powder flew all over the place. A couple of kids wrote "Cheer" on scraps of notebook paper: their reasonable facsimiles.

I grabbed my sign from the closet and rushed out on my front porch to see the Cheer Man pull up and stop directly in front of my house. I thought, He's really here!

As the Cheer Man got out of his car, I proudly held my sign high over my head. My heart was beating so hard I thought my chest would burst. Among a yardful of kids screaming for his attention, he spotted the giant, colored Cheer sign that I had worked so hard to make, walked over, and, with a big grin, said, "*You* get the ten dollars."

My parents were amazed—but in profoundly different ways. My father stood there agog, not quite believing his eyes, but happy for me, and my mother had a huge loving smile on her face. Until then, Sammy's Cheer sign had been a joke, and I was just this precocious bookworm of a kid who believed in the oddest things—like, for instance, that anything can happen if you just believe hard enough.

When the Cheer Man handed me the check for ten dollars, my father said, "How is this possible? How is it that you would come to this tiny town in this obscure part of Mississippi?"

The Cheer Man said, "Well, it's really very interesting. We have this thing called a 'computer.'" None of us knew anything about computers, except for the room-sized behemoths with flashing lights that made whirring and beeping noises in science fiction movies.

He went on, "The names of every registered voter, in every county, in every state in these United States were put into that computer. The computer picked two random addresses in every county in every state. 405 South Third Street in Amory was one of the two chosen in Monroe County, Mississippi, and it's just taken us this long to get down here."

Then he got back into his car and drove off.

I immediately rushed to the Security Bank of Amory, cashed the check—which was made out to "Resident of 405 South Third Street, Amory, Mississippi"—and bought three model airplanes, glue, and paint. I spent all of Labor Day weekend building those planes. Then I hung them from my ceiling and put them on the shelves in my room. Of course, today I wish my parents had just given me the ten dollars in cash and let me frame that check for posterity.

———

When the Cheer Man came to my hometown, just like the commercial had promised, I learned a very valuable lesson about the power of believing in a dream no matter how impossible it seems. *Anything* is possible. Everything my mother taught me, and everything that I promised to always strive for, is built on the idea that you should never give up on your dreams. And if your dreams come true, it just confirms and strengthens your faith for the next one.

I'm not saying that faith alone can make a dream come true. Faith isn't a magical power and there are no guarantees in life. But think of it this way: If you had to choose between feeling positive or negative, which is the more attractive choice? I'd rather feel good and work for the best result in something than be cynical and, if my dream still happened to come true, shrug my shoulders and think I got lucky just that one time. And if my dream didn't come true, rather than give up, I'd want to find the strength to move on to the next dream.

I guess what I'm saying is that faith—call it a souped-up version of the power of positive thinking—*is its own reward.* Believing that anything can happen is a forward-thinking mental state. It feels good. Then, as with a stone tossed into a pond, the ripple effect of your attitude not only radiates into the world, but it attracts like-minded people who might help you achieve your dreams, as well as those who want to feel as good as you do.

You are what you do. When a situation can go either way, having faith might just be that little bit of extra focus and energy and action it takes to make your dream come true.

———

My mother demonstrated this faith every day in ways both large and small. When I was a boy, whenever we'd see a penny on the street, she'd say: "See a penny, pick it up, and all the day you'll have good luck." It may seem corny, but it is a perfect example of my mother's insistence on finding good everywhere.

Since then, if I see a penny, I pick it up, and if I'm in the midst of a worrying situation, I say, "This is for that worry," and I believe that helps the worry go away. I pick up pennies everywhere. I will not pass one by. (Well, I did once, when I saw it in a urinal. I just couldn't do it.) I have been in a full tuxedo in a rainstorm and have bent down to snatch one out of a gutter as water rushed over it. The penny is symbolic. It reminds me to never forget my mother or that my journey started in Amory, Mississippi, where I was raised, and that it's always better to believe in a wonderful moment of luck than ignore it.

I believed in the Cheer Man, and he came. I was lucky because I got to experience firsthand the connection between faith and a positive outcome when I was still young enough for the moment to take deep root in me. It was as if someone had flipped on an inner light, and that light never went off. Today, I can't imagine feeling any other way.

Had the Cheer Man never come, though, I would simply have moved on to another dream. My mother would have made sure of that. As she often said, "When God closes a door he always opens a window." Fortunately, as my life went on, I was blessed with the success that came with so many of my dreams: I got to be who I wanted to be and not who others expected me to be, which meant moving to Los Angeles and working in show business, among other things. I married the woman I wanted to; I had two wonderful children to whom I can pass on lessons about the power of faith. Those were the big dreams. I also dreamed of winning the Good Citizenship Award in the eighth grade, of being Amory's youngest Eagle Scout, and of making the varsity football team in high school.

I'll say it again: It always pays to believe that good things *can* happen. Because the Cheer Man came to my house, I have to believe there's always hope.

Today, I still have the determined optimism of a ten-year-old boy whose mother never said a word to dash or damage his dreams, and whose faith in me has become my faith in myself. Both allow me to walk just a little bit taller in life.

In fact, the Cheer Man has come for me many times since. He still comes.

He can come for you, too, if you just believe.

Promises I Made My Mother

ONE

Promises I Made My Mother

A man loves his sweetheart the most, his wife the best, but his mother the longest. —IRISH PROVERB

Everybody needs their mother.

Mothers do more than give us life. They embrace, nourish, and comfort us. They are our first teachers, protectors, and guides. Our mothers are our conscience and our safe harbor. The mother/son relationship is not often written about, but my mother believed it is one of the strongest bonds that exists. As the poet Robert Browning put it, "Motherhood: All love begins and ends there."

My mother, Mary Kirkpatrick Haskell, was all of this and more to me. Her life was an inspiration. She graduated from high school in 1942, when she was only sixteen, as class valedictorian. She was also editor in chief of the school newspaper, class secretary, a Hall of Fame member, and the Daughters of the American Revolution Good Citizenship Girl of the Year. Her high school yearbook says it all: "She has a smile for every joy, a tear for every sorrow, an excuse for every fault, and an encouragement for every hope."

After high school my mother planned on going to college. A child of the Depression, she had big dreams about a bright and successful future, but because there was no money, she put aside that dream for a while and became a teller at the Bank Of Amory. Even there, her dedication attracted attention. Her looks did, too. My mother had big brown eyes, the most beautiful smile, rosy cheeks, auburn hair, and was thin with a real pretty figure. She reminded some of a young Jane Wyman. A neighbor, Mr. Guy Pickle, remembered how my mother used to walk home from the bank at lunchtime: "Every day all the businessmen on Main Street gathered just to watch your mother walk by. She was so beautiful she could stop running water."

My mother dreamed of leaving Amory, earning a nursing degree, and traveling the world. Without faith in herself, and trusting that her dreams could become a reality, she might have settled for less. But she persevered through good times and bad, and became both accomplished and respected in her profession as a school nurse practitioner and as a homemaker raising three boys. My mother had more friends than anyone else I've ever known. She was decent and kind to a fault, and she set me on the path to a positive life. Plus, she told me every day that I was special, and encouraged *my* dreams.

It might sound as if I've put her on a pedestal, but, of course, no one is perfect. Momma was sometimes too sensitive and a bit shy. But I loved her beyond all measure, and have never made a secret of it.

More than once I've been asked, "How could you love your mother that much?" I always answer, "How could I not?"

Simply put, my mother's life set an example for me, and the

lessons I learned from her are a part of everything I've done. After high school, I attended Ole Miss, where I met Mary Donnelly, the woman I'd soon marry. After graduation, I followed my show business dreams and in 1978 moved to Los Angeles, where I got my start in the mailroom of the prestigious William Morris Agency. Eighteen months later, I became a full-fledged talent agent and eventually represented a wide range of artists including Kathie Lee Gifford, Debbie Allen, Dolly Parton, Ray Romano, Bill Cosby, George Clooney, Whoopi Goldberg, Lily Tomlin, and His Royal Highness the Prince Edward. I became the agent for many talented writers, producers, and directors as well. I worked hard and eventually rose to become Worldwide Head of Television at William Morris—one of the most powerful jobs in Hollywood. When I resigned from the agency in December of 2004, after twenty-six years, Mary and I continued our journey focusing on philanthropic causes, several of which you will read about in this book.

None of this could have happened had I not taken to heart the many lessons my mother taught me daily, and worked to keep the many promises I made to her about how I'd live my life, promises large and small, spoken and silent, promises that brought me success and kept me grounded.

Because of my mother, I promised to share my blessings, have faith in myself, be kind, find something to believe in, treat everyone—high or low—the same, be a strong and fair parent, never stop dreaming, be a good friend, keep God at the center of my life, maintain my character and integrity, be trustworthy, live every day to the fullest, always pick up a penny for good luck, have a wonderful life, and never forget how much she loved me.

This book is about those promises.

Mary Nell Kirkpatrick was born in Amory, Mississippi, on July 17, 1925, the third child of Mary Katherine and Hezkiah Kirkpatrick. She had two brothers, James and Eugene, who were twelve and ten years older, respectively. They took her everywhere, not only to show off their beautiful little sister, but to teach her about the world. Grandmother Kirkpatrick (Nanny) welcomed the help, especially four years later when my aunt Betty was born—and the stock market crashed.

During those dark days in rural Mississippi, life was as bleak as we've all heard, but my mother's parents smothered their children with love, and they didn't really know just how poor they were. Still, they would have been much worse off had my grandfather not been one of the last Main Street blacksmiths in Mississippi. People had to shoe their plow and transportation horses even though they couldn't afford shoes for themselves.

My mother quickly learned that what little income her parents had was always shared. "Your grandmother was a wonderful cook, and known as one of the kindest women in Amory," she told me more than once. "During the Great Depression, she would always prepare three times as much food as was needed— for every meal—because the railroad ran right through town and hoboes would show up looking for work and something to eat. Because of her generosity, word spread and they found their way to your grandparents' house, where your aunt Betty and I would serve Momma's soup. There were never less than a dozen of them in our yard almost every day."

The lesson stuck, and my mother passed it on to me. "A blessing is not a blessing unless it is shared," she said again and again, making me and my brothers promise to do the same by encouraging us to tithe at church and spend several hours a week doing community service.

After working at the Bank of Amory for a year, my mother

landed a scholarship with the Air Force Cadet Nursing Corps to attend the University of Tennessee School of Nursing. Having been born with a "servant's heart," she felt a career in nursing would be the perfect way to help others. The country was in the midst of World War II, and when she graduated the Air Force sent her to a base hospital on Long Island, in New York. There she met two doctors, both of whom wanted to marry her. Dr. Frank Johnson was a boisterous, handsome, aggressive extrovert, my mother's opposite. Dr. Warren Nasiff was attractive, but quiet and shy. She chose Dr. Johnson, believing that opposites attract and that their personalities would complement each other. Of course, she was also madly in love with him. Dr. Johnson had also gotten an Air Force education, so after the wedding, which took place in Amory, at my grandparents' home, the newlyweds moved to Mobile, Alabama, where both were stationed at Brookley Air Force Base.

Everyone told my mother she had found "the perfect man," but they didn't know about Dr. Johnson's dark side. My mother did, but she'd discovered it too late and was too afraid to say anything. Frank Johnson was mentally and physically abusive to her. He would always apologize, but the cruelty continued. She endured silently for seven years, but after her second miscarriage she bravely stood up, told her parents, got a lawyer, and divorced him. All she asked for in the settlement was her home, and a new beginning.

A year after the divorce, my mother became head nurse at Brookley Air Force Base Hospital. The Korean War was under way, and by the summer of 1954 hundreds of boys were being flown into Brookley for care. One was Staff Sergeant Sam Haskell, Jr., from Cincinnati, Ohio. He had a broken leg. His room was on my mother's floor.

My mother later told me that "this very handsome young man

kept pushing the button at his bedside, asking for a nurse, but none would suit him." None, that is, until she walked in. My father confessed to me that he was smitten from the beginning and just wanted to meet her; he'd been going through all the nurses, looking for her. My mother was also dazzled, but, hurt by the failure of her first marriage, she was wary. My father had to pursue her and convince her to marry him.

It didn't take long. My parents got serious quickly and eloped on October 13, 1954.

My father was twenty-five and my mother was twenty-nine.

My father was charming, good-looking, and funny. He came from a blue-blood Ohio family and had a self-confidence that shone brightly. He could walk into any room and in five minutes you'd think he was the most fabulous guy ever. He'd been the star of his high school football and track teams. Everyone was drawn to him. I've seen pictures of my father in his late teens and early twenties: He looked like a movie star.

My father got a job as a clothing salesman, and my mother—who got pregnant right away—kept working at the base hospital, and waited for me to arrive. But when she was six months along there were complications. Fearing a third miscarriage, her obstetrician, Dr. John Hope, put her to bed for the duration.

I was born three weeks earlier than expected, at 6 P.M. on June 24, 1955. It couldn't have been easy for her. A few hours into her labor, Dr. Hope discovered I was a breech baby. Cesarean sections weren't as common in the mid-1950s as they are now, and he prepared my parents for a long and difficult delivery. Finally, after almost twenty-four hours and many large doses of pain medication, I arrived. After two miscarriages, my mother was thrilled to have given birth at all. She said she'd never felt such joy as when she heard me cry for the first time.

Then she did something totally unexpected. Once she was alert, she had Dr. Hope help her off the delivery table. He held her weak little body as she got down on her knees and gave me back to God, saying, "Take this boy and use him for thy will."

Over the next two years, she had my brothers Jamie and Billy. Those pregnancies were much easier, but she thanked God for my brothers' safe arrivals just the same.

Momma told me the story of my birth when I was twelve years old. By then she'd also told me every day, as far back as I can remember, that I was a special child, a blessing to her. I wanted to live up to her expectations. She said she was proud of the young man I had become, and the man she knew I would eventually be. And just to make sure that I continued to "stand in the light," she asked me to promise to learn and practice the lessons and principles she insisted would guide me to the light of God's goodness and grace, and help me find happiness and success and inner peace.

Because my father made good money, my mother was able to interrupt her nursing career to invest everything in raising her family. She was completely present in her sons' lives, there for us in every way, including milk and cookies (really!) every day when we got home from grade school. In the winter months, Momma would make us Campbell's Tomato Soup and a grilled cheese sandwich—my absolute favorite. I loved the jingle for the Campbell's Soup commercial . . . "Soup and Sandwich, Soup and Sandwich, have your favorite Campbell's Soup and Sandwich, any time or weather, Soup and Sandwich go together" . . . and I believed it! When we were a few years older she took a job as the first school nurse in Amory and helped pioneer the state's school nursing program. And best of all, she said, was that working for the school gave her the same holidays as her children.

And yet, as perfect a life as my mother tried to provide for us, our family still faced the same problems that everyone does. This became more apparent to me as I emerged from the cocoon of childhood innocence. In short, after ten good years, my parents' marriage began to crumble. What had once worked as the complement of two distinct personalities deteriorated into the relentless clash of two different temperaments.

Also, since I was his firstborn son, my father—as does every father—had a dream for my life. But what he wanted for my future (becoming a doctor) was not what I wanted, and the older I got the more conflict emerged as we both confronted that reality. My parents divorced after sixteen years of marriage, and I, like a lot of children of broken homes, felt forced to pick a side. I chose my mother. Subsequently, and despite all the good qualities my father had, there was no turning back to establish the kind of intimacy we both might have liked. It's a shame that my father left us, but I feel very lucky to have had a mother who, on her own, could raise me and my brothers as well as she did.

Today, I realize that I'm just an ordinary man who's been lucky enough to have lived an extraordinary life. I couldn't have done it without my mother's guidance, and I'm thankful for it every day. I was incredibly fortunate that she nurtured me so positively at the tender age when children are still open to all of the possibilities that the world has to offer. And because of her love and care I grew up determined to always act according to her faith in me and never disappoint her.

The promises I made my mother have always been at the center of my life.

TWO

Character Is All You Have in the Dark

Character cannot be developed in ease and quiet. Only through the experience of trial and suffering can the soul be strengthened, ambition inspired, and success achieved. —HELEN KELLER

Always let character be your guide. —MARY KIRKPATRICK HASKELL

My mother grew up during a time when people had few material possessions, so her character and reputation were her most valuable assets. She nurtured and guarded them with her every breath. Character is the rock on which my mother built her life, and she passed that value on to me. It is the foundation that supports everything else.

To some, character means integrity. Selflessness. The ability to inspire. Kindness. I think character is simply a unique combination of mental and moral qualities that distinguish us from one another. The Boy Scout Law best describes the complete recipe for good character: "Trustworthy, loyal, helpful, friendly, courteous, kind, obedient, cheerful, thrifty, brave, clean, and reverent." Character tells us most of what we want to know about someone, but more important, what's *essential* to know.

Here's how to tell: In the absolute dark, you can't tell if a person you meet is good-looking, plain, tall, short, fat, or thin. You don't know eye or hair color, or if they have any hair at all. You can't judge them by their clothes or body language. In fact, the only way to really assess who they are is by what they say and, more important, by how they act.

When you take away everything, when you strip a person of the superficial add-ons, all they have left is their true self. Character is what gives a person meaning. Character is the core of our being.

I first learned about character where we all do: at home. Since my father traveled often for work, my mother embraced the chance to show me the way.

HONESTY

Momma expected nothing less than honesty from all her sons, and she never missed an opportunity to teach us the importance of always telling the truth.

My mother loved to read, and she worked hard to instill that same passion in her children. When Jamie, Billy, and I were little boys, my mother took us to the nearby Amory Municipal Library every Saturday. In the '50s and early '60s, the library was housed in the City Hall, a large old building from the '30s. The outside walls were smooth concrete, and the inside smelled of history. I loved walking between the stacks looking at the newest selections, and I also loved the more timeworn volumes. Often, I would open those old books and read the names on the card that revealed who had read the book before me.

When I was eight years old, my mother thought I was mature enough to walk to the library by myself and be responsible for checking out and returning my own books. That meant I got to have my own library card, which made me feel so grown-up.

I have always loved English history, and one Saturday I rushed to the library to check out a new book on the kings and queens of England. When I got home to show my mother the book, she asked if I had returned the books I'd checked out the week before. I hadn't, but I lied and told her that I had. I knew those books were still in my bedroom, but I figured that I could put them in my book satchel and drop them off at the library on my way home from school on Monday.

Unfortunately, I forgot the books on Monday, and the next day, and the next day as well. Soon they were buried in my room under boxes of model cars and airplanes, baseball cards, parts of a Monopoly board, a kite with a tail made from old pillowcases, and my GI Joe paraphernalia—and there they remained for several months. Imagine my surprise when my mother received a notice in the mail from the library inquiring about my books—*and* there was *a late fee charge of eight dollars* . . . a lot of money in those days!

My mother marched me into my room and we started digging for the books. After we finally unearthed all four she walked me to the library, made me return the books, and made *me* pay the late fee with my own money. I had managed to save over ten dollars from my fifty-cent-a-week allowance, and in a flash it was almost all gone.

"Honesty means owning your mistakes," my mother said. "And apologizing for them." Before we left the library, I had to apologize to the librarian for keeping the books out for so long and promise my mother to never be dishonest again.

———

That lesson stuck—I was always good about library books from then on! But there were other kinds of dishonesty that I hadn't yet learned to avoid. When I was a high school sophomore, my cousin Nan Elliott, my friend Debbie Morris, and I would get together every night and study for our world history class. Well, sort of study. Actually, we'd laugh and tell stories until midnight, while my mother came in every half hour with snacks, asking, "Now, are you kids studying?" We'd all nod our heads and assure her we were.

When the girls went home, I'd stay up the rest of the night poring through my books so I could still make the A. I don't think Nan and Debbie did. One day in class, I squished down low in my chair so Nan and Debbie could look over my shoulder and compare their answers with the answers on my test paper. When I looked up, there was our teacher, Jane Lancaster, standing right over me. "You seem to be slouching today, Mr. Haskell," she said.

For some reason, I burst out laughing. Then Nan and Debbie started to laugh. Though it was so unlike any of us to pull that kind of stunt, we couldn't stop.

Mrs. Lancaster didn't laugh. Instead, she gave me a look that froze me. She didn't have to let the incident slide, but she did. At that moment I realized that while your mother might always forgive you, the world doesn't have to. All anyone has is their reputation, which is easy to shatter and difficult to repair. I was put on notice that I'd been lucky to keep mine. Nan, Debbie, and I still remember the moment as one of the funniest things that happened to us in high school, but the lesson stuck.

———

Eight years later, after moving to Los Angeles, I worked in the William Morris Agency mailroom. My salary was $125 a week, *before* taxes, so I also had a part-time job at Professor Bloodgood's Olde Time Photography Shoppe, on the Universal Studios tour, taking pictures of tourists dressed up as movie stars or gangsters or Western saloon people.

When I tell you that I had no money in those early days, it is a fact. Each Sunday night, I would purchase only what I needed to make my lunch for five days. For ten dollars, I could buy enough bread, ham, and cheese to make five ham and cheese sandwiches. I could also get one large bag of potato chips, which I'd divide evenly into five Ziploc bags. And I'd get a six-pack of Coca-Cola.

Yet every day at work I was surrounded by food—and temptation. I'd have to drive to the market to pick up Danish, fruit, lox, bagels, and sumptuous lunches for the agents. I was given the money to pay for the food, and I would give the change to the mailroom clerk. Another trainee who did the market run with me said that he and some of the other guys would order more food than was really needed and leave some groceries in their cars to take home. I saw him do it several times, and he suggested I do the same. Maybe it seems like no big deal to some people— you know, I'm just one guy and the company can afford it—but as much as I needed and wanted that food, I remembered the promise I had made to my mother about valuing my reputation and self-respect, and said, "No, that's not honest."

Good character, my mother had always explained, meant never letting yourself go anywhere you can't come back from. Don't do something you can't retract. Don't make the fatal error. Don't delude yourself that something wrong is right because you *wish* it were right because life is unfair. If I had been comfortable stealing a quart of tuna fish, who knows what else I might have eventually gotten comfortable with?

My partner on the market run was astounded—angry even— and froze me out with some of the other guys as someone who didn't play along. Was he ashamed of himself, or worried that I might spill the beans, or both? I know I spent the next few days wondering if I'd been ostracized because my refusal to cheat had seemed too judgmental about what the other trainees did to get by.

It didn't matter. I still couldn't do it and feel morally straight. Damage to a person's character can start with the smallest crack in the mirror. So I ignored their attitudes and focused on my work. I also vowed that if, in the years to come, the business ever required me to do something that made it difficult to look at myself in the mirror because I'd not been true to what I knew was right, I would not and could not continue doing it.

Today, I believe that turning down that minor opportunity to take what wasn't mine helped me prevail when far more consequential temptations and compromises presented themselves—as they inevitably do. Since then, I have eaten in some of the world's finest restaurants, yet there is still something special to me about a ham and cheese sandwich, a handful of potato chips, and a Coke.

HONORING THE CHARACTER OF OTHERS

I have always dearly loved my first cousins Dan and Mary Rogers. Dan was two years older than I, and Mary was three years younger, but my mother and my aunt Betty raised Dan and Mary along with me and my brothers, Jamie and Billy, as if we were siblings.

Because Dan was older, I always looked up to him, wanted to be like him, and of course, wanted him to like me. Mary was the little sister I had always wanted. I adored her. Still do. When we were kids, we all lived just minutes away from each other, so we always played together after school and on weekends. When I was eight and Dan was ten, Dan started having after-school football games in his backyard, and I wanted to play. Unfortunately, he had grown a bit weary of his younger "shadow"—me. Also, I was not as good at sports as the other boys, and Dan was probably a little embarrassed about my lack of ability. One day, we got into an argument about why I couldn't play with him and his friends, and he pulled out his BB gun and shot me several times in the rear end. I ran home in tears, and just as I was telling my mother what had happened, Aunt Betty and Dan arrived at our back door. Aunt Betty had immediately found out what had happened, and she had brought Dan to our house to apologize. I was still crying, very angry, and I didn't want to accept his apology. Dan, however, knew what he had to do, and even though he might have done it reluctantly, with my mother and Aunt Betty watching, he tried to apologize. I pouted and turned away. Suddenly, my mother took me by the shoulders and said, "Sammy, it takes a big man to apologize, but it takes a bigger man to accept it."

Realizing that she was right, I grudgingly shook his hand and accepted Dan's apology. Looking back, I realize that my relationship with Dan turned an important corner that day. We went through Boy Scouts together, high school football together, and Ole Miss together, and he was a groomsman in my wedding. Because he'd been big enough to apologize and I'd understood the meaning of honoring his character by accepting that apology, he became the big brother that I wished I'd always had.

———

It's funny how even years later those lessons stick with you. By the time I had worked my way up to become Worldwide Head of the Television Department at William Morris, I found myself in the parental role, hoping that an agent in my department would have the character to apologize for and own a mistake he'd made.

I had asked him to submit an actress client of mine for a role in a TV miniseries. After three days of waiting for a meeting to be scheduled, I'd heard nothing. The actress called me on the hour, wondering what had happened, and I kept calling the agent to find out when the meeting would be set. When I finally got my agent on the phone, he told me that the producers had passed and would not agree to meet my client.

I was shocked, so I called the producer myself. He said he had never spoken to my agent about the matter.

My practice was to always back my team, and in the rare instance I discovered I had an internal problem, to handle it immediately. When agents had problems with each other, I'd get them to trade apologies, find a common ground, and then move on. In this case, I set up my client's meeting with the producer myself, then called the responsible agent into my office. I told him what the producer had said, and asked him to clarify what had happened. His answer: "You caught the producer in a lie, and he must have agreed to the meeting to placate you."

I knew the agent was lying to save face. The producer had been a friend for twenty years; he had no reason to lie to me. The whole situation could have been dismissed with a warning if my agent had just done the right thing and apologized. But unlike my cousin Dan, he didn't. I didn't fire him, but it caused me to question his character from that day forward.

HARD WORK

Thanks to my mother's lessons and examples, I was a pretty good kid growing up, as these things go. I knew the difference between right and wrong. I wanted to make my parents proud. I made mostly straight As in school. I was respectful and kind. I was involved in community service and church activities. I had leads in the school plays and musicals. I was an Eagle Scout, Rotary Boy of the Year, senior class president, Class Favorite, and member of the Hall of Fame.

And yet, I felt a constant need to be liked by everyone around me.

Sports were one path to popularity. I knew that would also please my father, who had excelled at football and track and loved the jocular, go-drink-with-the-boys-and-watch-a-ball-game camaraderie.

I enjoyed tennis and swimming. I disliked football, baseball, and track.

Helping with charities and working at the church made me feel good about myself.

Dad thought I should be working out in the gym.

My father made me join Little League when I was eight. I couldn't throw well and didn't bat well. He figured that maybe I'd pick up a few skills as well as get some fresh air and physical conditioning, and I did it because my mother had taught me to handle any responsibility to the best of my ability. Commitment not only built character, she said, but resulted in success. Often she'd quote the Book of Luke: "To those whom much is given, much is required." I understood, and so I threw myself into whatever sports made my father happy, and I was determined to go above and beyond the call of duty.

Through hard work and some well-timed growth spurts, I improved. In middle school I played football and I was on the swim team. In high school I was on the tennis team and on the Amory Panther varsity football team as a starting lineman for two years. As a senior, I was even chosen as a cocaptain for one of our Friday night games.

That wasn't quite enough for my father. He also wanted me to be a track star, as he'd been. Obediently, I joined the track team even though I hated running, a truth I'd discovered when the football coach made the squad run after spring practice. We'd run a couple of miles up and back on Highway 25 North, which connected Amory to the little town of Smithville. There were no lights on Smithville Road. One night, after a really rough football practice, I was late exchanging my cleats for tennis shoes and getting out of my pads and into my running gear. I managed to keep up for the first couple of miles, but on the way back, I slowed down as it got darker and darker. Because we weren't allowed to walk, I trotted. Slowly. I passed a house with a big, well-lit front yard, and a barking dog jolted me "awake." When it ran at me, I started running as fast as I could—which wasn't very. The dog caught up with me and bit my ankle. The owner rushed out, grabbed his dog, and said, "I thought everybody had gone by twenty minutes ago. That's why I let the dog out. You sure can't run very fast, can you, boy?"

I hung in there, but I realized I would never be much of a runner. However, my throwing all my effort into football did please my father and made me feel good about myself—especially because as an offensive lineman, I didn't have to run very much (unless it was backpedaling furiously to protect the quarterback).

———

The persistence and commitment to hard work that I'd learned as a child came in handy early on at William Morris. While in the mailroom, I kept my second job at Professor Bloodgood's Olde Time Photography Shoppe on weekends. Having no days off for almost an entire year was exhausting, but it had to be done. Thank goodness I was young enough—twenty-three—and had the energy to match my ambition. And I didn't mind working my butt off because, beginning with the Cheer Man experience, I had faith that the rewards would come as long as I put in the effort.

In the mailroom, I was always the first to volunteer for the most menial chores. As the most famous William Morris mailroom graduate, David Geffen, has said, "The work was more tedious than it was tough. I had to change the toilet paper in the bathrooms and fill the soap dispensers. It wasn't challenging, just what I had to do to get to the next step—and I was always willing to do that. . . . The mailroom is where you learn that if you haven't got the patience to go through the s**t, you're not going to get to the cream. It's a test. It's about humility. Lots of people complained, though, and quit because they thought it was demeaning. I kept hoping everybody would quit, because the more people who quit, the higher up on the list I got toward [getting out of the mailroom]." One merely has to look at the heights that David Geffen reached as an agent, personal manager, art collector, moviemaker, and cofounder of DreamWorks Pictures to understand the wisdom of his advice.

One task that could get you noticed at William Morris, and perhaps lead to a promotion, was to read three movie scripts a night and then deliver typed-up synopses of each the next morning. I once took an assignment to read scripts the night of the Academy Awards; I had to stay up until six in the morning to get it all done. Or I might be asked to take the mail from Beverly Hills to Marina del Rey on a Friday night, through rush-hour traffic, when no one else would do it because they had hot dates.

But whether I delivered mail in the building or packages to movie studios and stars, I was determined to make an impression. Big smile. Always happy. Always eager. Too often we don't realize how important these little things—these brief connections—can be. I made sure everyone saw me working hard, because that was the way out of the mailroom and to a job as an assistant on an agent's desk.

I didn't get hired on the first agent's desk I tried for, but through a combination of opportunity, luck, and keeping my nose to the grindstone, I did get the second desk, working for Deborah Miller, about whom you'll learn more below.

My second week at William Morris, I had delivered mail to a man named Sy Sussman, who ran the screening room. While looking at the projection equipment, I realized it was the same setup we used at the Ole Miss TV station. When Mr. Sussman decided to take his vacation, he said, "Mr. Lastfogel [the big boss!] comes in every afternoon to watch an old movie. I need someone up here who can operate this equipment."

I said, "Well, I can do it." So he pulled me out of the mail-room for a week and I ran the projection room. I had read about Abe Lastfogel in Garson Kanin's book on Hollywood, so I took advantage of the chance to make an important connection and have a short chat with him each afternoon, and impress him with my knowledge of Hollywood history.

During my week running the screening room, my future boss, Deborah Miller, came to watch a tape of a TV special starring her client Ann-Margret—who later became my client—with the Radio City Music Hall Rockettes. Ms. Miller was head of the television variety department, which put together specials and handled bookings on all the award shows. At that time *The Donny and Marie Show* was very popular, as was *Battle of the Network Stars*. And there were dozens of TV talk shows.

After the tape was finished, Deborah asked for my opinion. She agreed with what I had to say, and it turned out she later shared my comments with the show's producer. That started our relationship. At the same time I regularly talked to her assistant, Amy Howard, and always pointed out, "I'd really like to work for Ms. Miller one day." When Amy was promoted, Deborah Miller took me out of the mailroom, where I'd been for only nine months, and put me on her desk.

I knew my mother would be proud of how my hard work had paid off—and she was. Plus, she loved the stories I could tell her about my "adventures" with the stars, especially when they gave me the chance to put her lessons to work.

For instance, one of Deborah's clients was Doc Severinsen, the bandleader on *The Tonight Show Starring Johnny Carson*. Doc's manager was Bud Robinson. Bud and his wife, Cece, had been very nice to me, inviting me to parties at their home, taking me to dinner, teaching me about the entertainment business. Suddenly, Cece was diagnosed with cancer, and had to be admitted to Cedars Sinai hospital in Beverly Hills. To cheer her up I decided to write a story, complete with funny photos cut out of a magazine with pictures of my head put on other people's bodies. I asked Bud if I could visit Cece and bring what I'd written. He said absolutely. When I walked into her hospital room there was Johnny Carson and his wife, Joanna. I froze. How could I possibly perform my silly little story in front of the King of Comedy? I stalled, I hemmed and hawed, and finally Cece said, "Sam, Bud told me you've written something for me."

"Yes, ma'am," I said.

Joanna Carson and Bud egged me on to read the story, while Mr. Carson sat there silently. I had to do it. It took about five minutes to read the story and pass the funny photos around the room. Cece smiled and gave me a hug. Then a voice I knew all too well piped up: "Maybe you should have opened in a smaller hospital—out of town."

The room exploded in laughter.

Not long after that, I got another chance to actually *show* my mother the progress I'd made. David Letterman was also Deborah's client, and occasionally she'd send me to take care of him when he guest-hosted for Johnny Carson on *The Tonight Show*. But on his very first night guest-hosting, we both went with him. In the dressing room, he didn't like the way his suit and tie looked. He glanced at me and said, "Haskell, your tie is perfect. Let me have it." I did. Then I called my mother to say, "Be sure and watch *The Tonight Show*. David Letterman's wearing that tie you gave me last Christmas."

HUMILITY

Be proud of yourself but remember, There's no indispensable man.
—"THE INDISPENSABLE MAN," SAXON WHITE KESSINGER

As I have mentioned, I wanted very much to be liked as a young man. I still have a hard time accepting that someone I hope likes me doesn't—and that sometimes I can't do anything about it no matter how hard I try. I've occasionally been told by those closest to me, "You want everyone to love you so much that you'll do anything to make it happen."

They are probably right. I may be blessed with a positive, can-do outlook, but still, no one wants to live with situations in which they can't-do.

My mother warned me about this conundrum, but it took many years before I could accept that not everyone would see me as I wanted them to. I understood it intellectually, and life was fine as long as I didn't run into someone who actively disliked me, but when I did, and all attempts to open or change their mind failed, I hated the powerless feeling in the pit of my stomach.

Knowing how much I wanted approval, my mother recognized the sometimes unwitting lengths I'd go to to get it, like announcing my grand plans to anyone and everyone. I had a habit of saying, "When I grow up I'm going to be . . ." or "When I'm in senior high school I'm going to be . . ." Lots of kids say that, and my excitement was truly that of an innocent child. My mother could have smiled at what I said and patted me reassuringly on the head, believing I'd come up with something completely different the next day. Or she could have tried to protect me from disappointment and embarrassment by telling me to be more realistic about my dreams, not to mention more humble. Instead, my mother saw these moments as opportunities to focus my behavior on *actually achieving those goals*. She recognized a chance to help me learn that actions were more powerful than words. She understood that the hard work I'd endure would help me learn humility naturally. So she decided to take an active role in putting me in charge of building my own character and integrity.

For example, in the fifth grade, after the annual school awards ceremony, I told my mother, "When I'm in the eighth grade I'm going to win the school's Good Citizenship Award."

"Before you win that award in the eighth grade, you've got to be a good citizen *today*," she said. "You're going to have to do something every day, every week, every year, until the award is given. You can *decide* you're going to win it, but winning it is more than just a decision. You've got to work for it—starting now."

I did what Momma said to do, and three years later, at the beginning of my eighth-grade year, I decided that it might help my grand plan if I was elected middle school student body president. Every kid from the fifth to eighth grade could vote. When I told my mother, she said, "How are you going to plan this?"

Unfortunately, I wasn't the most popular boy in the eighth grade, though at times I thought I was. My teachers loved me, and I had the principal's respect. I was so pleased with what I saw when I looked in the mirror that I was, frankly, cocky, and I believed that some of the kids who weren't that fond of me were actually just jealous.

Suspecting that I couldn't count on my eighth-grade peers to elect me, I decided my chances of winning might be better if I could convince most of the fifth grade to vote for me. My best friend, Randy Hollis, and I made hundreds of "Vote for Sam" buttons on his Vac-U-Form where you pump and pump the heated contraption until the plastic sheets get soft on the mold that you want to create. Then my cousin Mary Rogers, a fifth grader, helped pass them out to her classmates. I won the election by a landslide! Everybody was astounded.

One day at lunch, flush with victory, I boasted, "I'm going to be president of the freshman, sophomore, and junior classes in high school, and as a senior, president of the student body." Then, looking at the friends who had gathered around, I nailed it with, "I'm going to need all of you to jump in and get involved."

I would soon learn that I should have listened to Momma and been a bit more humble—or at least quiet—about my big goals.

————

As the end of the eighth grade approached, I was totally psyched up for the annual all-school award day program at which my dream of winning the Good Citizenship Award would come true. Prior to that, in April, four other eighth graders and I had been chosen by the high school football coach to work out with his varsity team during spring training. This was an excellent chance for me to earn the respect of the older players, the attention of my future coaches, and my father's all-important approval.

In addition, through my extensive piano training, I had won superior ratings at three college piano festivals, and as such, I had been chosen to close the all-school talent show that took place on the Wednesday afternoon of the last week of spring training. My piano teacher, Mrs. Marilyn Nabors, was so proud.

The talent show started at 3:30 P.M., but since I was the closing act I didn't have to perform until 5:15. I convinced the high school football coach to let me leave practice early, at 4:30, so I could shower and change into my suit. My mother was set to pick me up at 5 and drive me the five minutes to my middle school. I was cutting it close, but I really wanted it all.

Unfortunately, during practice on talent show day, my coach forgot to tell me what time it was. When I saw my mother waving at me from the edge of the field, I realized it was 5. I ran to the locker room, took the quickest shower I've ever taken, threw on my suit, and, with my hair wet and sweat still pouring from my body, scrambled into the front seat of her aqua blue Chevrolet. Five minutes later, my mom pulled up in front of the middle school and told me to run for it while she parked the car.

I sprinted inside, only to be met by my very angry piano teacher.

"The principal is doing your introduction *now*," she said.

I had no time to collect my thoughts, say a prayer, or do anything, so I summoned as much confidence as I could and strode directly onstage. At least my wet hair had been "finger-combed" by my mother at every stop sign between the high school and the middle school.

Honestly, I wasn't that worried. I had played my piece a hundred times. The first chord involved all five fingers on both hands. It was meant to be a startling beginning. But after hitting that opening chord twice, I went completely blank. I could not for the life of me remember what followed. For the longest moment I just sat there in the deafening silence, until, frustrated, I lost control, banged the keys with both hands, and rushed off the stage. Then I went straight to the parking lot, laid my head on the hood of my mother's car, and cried.

My mother and my piano teacher rushed to the parking lot and found me. While my mother soothed me, Mrs. Nabors coolly suggested that maybe football and piano didn't mix.

I knew I had disappointed many people and made an idiot of myself. When I calmed down, I went inside and apologized to everyone, and decided that all I could do was look ahead two weeks to the Awards Day ceremony, and the prize I still felt certain I'd win.

A few days before the awards, our school principal, Dr. Holace Morris, traditionally called the parents of each winner to "secretly" reveal that their child would be honored. That way, the parents could sneak into the back of the auditorium and witness their child's special moment. Every day for a week before the awards, I called my mother at lunch and asked, "Mom, has Dr. Morris called yet? Have I won the Good Citizenship Award?"

Her reply was always the same: "No honey, he hasn't called. I'm sure he'll call tomorrow."

On Awards Day, I dressed for school and rehearsed what I'd say in my acceptance speech. I had decided that my mom knew I'd won, but wanted me to be surprised—which is why she hadn't told me about Dr. Morris's call. I put it out of my mind and went to classes. But right before the assembly, my anxiety got the better of me and I went to the school office and called my mother again.

"Momma," I said, "I promise I'll be surprised, but please just tell me that Dr. Morris has called."

"Sweetheart," she said, "he hasn't called. Maybe they're doing it differently this year, and not calling the parents. Remember last year, when the winner's name leaked out . . . ?"

Of course, I thought. Mom was always right.

But suddenly I caught myself wondering why she was still at home. Surely if I had won, someone would have made certain she'd be at the ceremony to celebrate.

On my way to the auditorium I noticed Weesie and Richard Hollis, my best friend Randy's parents, sneaking into the school through one of the back doors.

At that moment, I knew I had lost the award.

I went numb. I also realized that Randy probably didn't even care if he won the award—he was simply kind, polite, and well-adjusted. Everyone liked him; no one was jealous of him. At that moment, I realized he was the perfect boy to win.

I walked up to Dr. and Mrs. Hollis, in whose home I had spent half of my life, and I said, "Randy's won the Good Citizenship Boy of the Year, hasn't he?" The looks on their faces told me I was right. They hugged me and softly said, "Yes."

I knew they knew how I felt. I had told them many times about my dream of winning that award. Still, I hugged them back and said congratulations—then excused myself to hide with my disappointment in the boys' restroom.

As student body president, I had to speak at the end of the ceremony. Unfortunately, the speech I'd planned included my thanks to the teachers who had given me the award. What would I say now? I was good at thinking on my feet, but this was a situation I had never anticipated.

After Randy's name was announced, and the Good Citizenship Award given, I walked slowly to the podium. I tried to hold back the tears that I felt might burst through again at any moment. Desperate, I asked God for something to say, and luckily a poem came to mind that I had learned the year before for a church event, a poem my mother had taught me, one she'd learned thirty years earlier from her high school English teacher.

I stood before the faculty, the parents, and the students, gathered myself, congratulated every award recipient, then said: "If I should win, let it be by the code, with my faith and my honor held high, but if I should lose, let me be the first to stand by the road and cheer, as the winner walks by."

I wished everyone a great summer, and the program was over.

Afterward, I went straight to my favorite teacher's classroom. Mr. Mike Justice—his name reminded me of a superhero, and sometimes I thought of him that way. He was standing with his back to the door, cleaning the blackboard. Without looking to see who had walked in, he said, "Come in, Sam." He knew I would want to know why I didn't win "my award," and I knew Mr. Justice would tell me. He shook my hand, told me to sit in his desk chair, and explained that I had lost the Good Citizenship Award by only one vote.

"Why?" I asked.

"Because you banged the piano keys during the talent show, and stormed off the stage. Several teachers thought it was inappropriate behavior."

He was right. I thanked him for telling me the truth, which provided the understanding I needed to move ahead. My character had deserted me momentarily, and in public. My humility had been missing in action. I knew I'd have to work hard to be consistent, and I promised myself to always work to control my negative emotions.

But I still had a bigger lesson in humility to learn.

When ninth grade rolled around, I ran for freshman class president, as I'd planned.

I didn't even get into the runoff.

After losing the Good Citizenship Award, I had worked very hard to change and become a more humble, better person. I still had dreams, but I kept them mostly to myself instead of bragging about my grand designs in a way that annoyed everyone. Rather than assume the world should recognize my outstanding qualities, I now tried to help others succeed, and complimented people on *their* accomplishments. Instead of telling everyone what they should and should not do, now I asked my parents and brothers and friends what *they* thought *I* should do. Even if I still thought I had all the answers, I made myself seek others' opinions.

Although my personal evolution didn't make headlines, people *did* seem to like me more. I'd been taken down a notch in my own and my classmates' estimation, and having digested a big slice of humble pie, I acted more like a regular, old-fashioned teenager. I was more pleasant to be around. So why had I lost the election?

In tenth grade I ran for sophomore class president. Again, I missed the runoff.

One day I told my cousin Nan Elliott that I couldn't figure out what was going on. She finally broke the news. "Sam," she said, "remember that day in the eighth-grade lunchroom? Well, there were four or five girls who heard you say you were going to be president of every class and that they ought to pitch in now, and they pledged to do anything and everything they could to keep you from winning anything. They have been actively campaigning against you."

Boy, was that a comeuppance. One stupid statement, and its effect had lingered for years. In fact, I was not elected to office in high school until my junior year. Finally—and I credit this to being good at football—I was nominated and chosen as Class Favorite.

I didn't run for student body president my senior year, because I hadn't been on the student council, but I did run and win the office of senior class president. I never made a big deal about any of it. I just enjoyed the moment, with humility.

———

Losing the Good Citizenship Award was an early defining moment in my life. Until then, most everything had always gone my way. Losing the award was a valuable wake-up call—both in my self-perception and in my attitude toward others. In retrospect, I can see that I was at times a flawed and prideful thirteen-year-old. My mother had told me that to get what I wanted I had to start behaving like a winner immediately. I would learn that she didn't mean behave like someone who had *already* won—which is the mistake I'd made—but behave so consistently in keeping with the imagined end result that my character would shine through.

Once through that rite of passage, the young man I saw every day in the mirror began to assume a more solid shape. I was far from complete, but I had begun to define myself in the world on my own terms. I had begun to internalize the lessons of honesty, hard work, honoring others, and humility.

I had begun my journey toward a principled life.

THREE

Mirror Moments

When you get what you want in your struggle for pelf,
And the world makes you king for a day,
Just go to the mirror and look at yourself,
And see what that guy has to say.
For it isn't your father or mother or wife
Who judgment upon you must pass,
The feller whose verdict counts most in your life
Is the guy staring back from the glass.

—"THE GUY IN THE GLASS," PETER DALE WIMBROW, SR.

You can never be who you're going to be until you realize who you
are right now. If you like who you are, becoming who you'll be is easy.

—MARY KIRKPATRICK HASKELL

Fifteen years ago, following a motivational guest lecture I did about the business of show business at UCLA, a student asked me when I'd known what I really wanted to do. "Before I knew what I really wanted to do," I replied, echoing my mother's advice, "I had to know who I was."

We all start out trying to please our parents and family and teachers and friends. It's only natural. Whether we're in grade school, at a job, at a family gathering, or on vacation, we can't ignore taking cues from the approving or disapproving ways people react to us. In school, I had pushed myself in sports to please my father, to make myself "more of a man," and I had pushed myself with my music to please my mother because she loved the arts. The rest of the time I tried to please everyone else because I so desperately wanted them to like me. I loved the approval, but I served too many masters without serving the most important one: myself. In the end we have to give the greatest weight to how *we* feel, how we define *ourselves,* whether or not anyone else agrees or approves. Knowing who we are requires careful observation. We must look in the mirror often, both literally and figuratively, and have the strength of character to be honest with ourselves about what we see. Otherwise our lives become compromised and we are left forever incomplete.

Some people, tragically, never have these mirror moments. Some, when they do, can't decide who to be. Instead, they fall prey to the pressure of living in a fast-paced society in which everyone wants to be happy and successful, and they become men and women with many insincere faces: perky with one person and serious with another; nice to one and tough with someone else. They'll tell one person they like someone and tell another they dislike the same person. Instead of being honest, these people get caught up in presenting what they think *others* expect from them, hoping to find their identities and self-esteem by meeting those expectations. I certainly did that in school, trying to please everyone so they'd like me. It's an easy trap to fall into because it often seems as if society rewards those whose personalities can most fluidly respond to the expectations of others.

In fact, I believe it's the other way around. Society rewards consistency. We are our best selves when our personalities rest on a dependable *inner* definition and an *outer* execution of who we are.

You have to work at it. Our values and sense of self are challenged every day. It's difficult, given the conflicting demands of the modern world, to not lose or fragment your soul in the face of potentially compromising situations. But if you know and like what you see in the mirror, you have the best foundation on which to build a consistent character.

And here's more good news: Even though knowing, liking, and maintaining yourself can feel like an uphill battle, it's also transformative. You become a magnet of consistency to which the *inconsistent* personalities spinning around you are drawn. They want the order and success you exhibit in your life to be part of their lives.

Success comes if you're one person, true to yourself, and don't present yourself as anything different.

My mother was levelheaded, consistent, and inspirational. How could I not be drawn to someone like that? She supported me unconditionally, nurtured my search for self. She wanted me to realize my dreams. She understood that if I didn't act in accordance with what I saw in my mirror, my happiness would be at stake.

This came from her own experience. The one inconsistent situation at this stage of my mother's life was her marriage to my father. Whatever had attracted them to each other had been damaged by my father's relentless dissatisfactions. He was controlling and judgmental, and she could almost never make him happy.

A small example: Once, after my father had been away for a month on a business trip, my mother told our housekeeper, Oralee Small, "Mr. Haskell is going to check this house with a white glove when he returns. We've got to get everything clean, spick-and-span, and get dinner ready." It seemed horrible to me that everyone was so afraid of my father's judgment, but of course he judged me, too.

By the time he arrived, the house was perfect. Or so my mother thought. Turns out she'd forgotten to change the tinfoil that caught the grease under the eyes of the stove. He went right for it: "Damn it to hell, what's this dirty tinfoil doing under here?!" She broke into tears, ran to the bathroom, and locked herself in. I stood outside the door saying, "Momma, come out, it's okay." This went on, for one reason or another, for years.

In contrast to this, though, my mother showed that she could be incredibly strong during the most trying of situations.

In 1969, when I was fourteen years old, my father's good friend Nob Morris drove my father, my brothers, and me to a high school football game in Pontotoc, a town about an hour from Amory. I was tall and I dreaded riding in the backseat of Nob's little Thunderbird, crammed in with my brothers, but my father moved the front passenger seat up to give me more leg room. The roads weren't great, and on the way it got very foggy. As Nob came up over a hill near Okolona, he suddenly slammed into some cars that had just moments earlier been involved in a fatal accident.

No one wore seat belts in those days. Jamie and Billy were thrown onto the floorboard. Nob smashed his head and chest into the steering wheel. My father went headfirst through the passenger side of the windshield, and because I had squeezed in behind him, his seat crumpled forward and I went through the windshield right after him. The impact of the accident knocked me out.

When I woke up ten minutes later, my father was holding my head and crying, pleading with God to let me live. His hands were covered with blood from a gash across the side of my scalp.

Or so I thought. I looked up at my father, and what I saw still causes nightmares. Half of his face was torn off; blood was pouring out everywhere. I remember screaming, and then all of us were put into ambulances and taken to Okolona Hospital.

My mother got the call from the Mississippi Highway Patrol: "Your husband and your three sons have been in a fatal car crash." She later told me that she couldn't allow herself to think which one—if not all of us—she had lost, so my mother did what she always did in times of crisis: She dropped to her knees in prayer, and she called Aunt Betty and her husband, Hal Rogers.

Uncle Hal drove Momma and Aunt Betty to the hospital at 90 miles an hour. My mother found Jamie and Billy first. At the same time, Aunt Betty found me and yelled, "Mary Nell! Sammy is okay!" We were all on stretchers in little cubicles. As befits a nurse, my mother stayed unbelievably calm, insisting that the doctors call a plastic surgeon to help with my lacerations and my father's face. She was a pillar of strength and never cried. Her character shone so brightly that it comforted everyone else.

Nob had already been taken to Tupelo Medical Center with internal injuries. My brothers went home with Aunt Betty and Uncle Hal, and my father and I eventually followed Nob to Tupelo in an ambulance for observation. I got out the next afternoon.

My father stayed in the hospital for two weeks. During that time he had an epiphany of sorts, and apologized profusely to each of us for how harsh and critical he had always been of not only my brothers and me, but of my mother as well. For the first time in a long time I felt like I had a real family.

I thought he meant it, but what happened next required my mother to be even tougher than she had been that night in the emergency room.

The day my mother and I went to get my father from the hospital, an arrangement of yellow roses arrived. My mother asked me to gather all the flowers by his bedside and put them in the car—but not the yellow roses. I thought that was odd until, about two weeks later, we began to get calls at the house from a woman in Pensacola, Florida. The other woman.

Suddenly the reason for my father's long and then longer absences from his family became crystal clear.

I was angry. With perspective, I realized that my father had come to know himself, carrying within him the guilt of having an affair, and in order to like himself after staring death in the face, had had to apologize for all that he'd put us through. But he still could not come out and admit that he was no longer the person who had married my mother. He snuck around in the shadows with other women for years until *this* other woman, and then my mother, had the courage to make him choose. I wish he'd been honest with himself and his family sooner. I wanted my father to be happy, but I also wanted my family to stay together. I still think he turned his back on that second chance.

I've always found it hard to understand that such an evolved, brilliant woman as my mother made such poor choices in men, which just goes to prove that even the best of us are still human. But despite her troubles, in all other ways she remained consistent with the person she wanted to see when she looked into her mirror. Later, I understood that by redoubling her dedication to her nursing, and doing as much good as possible in the world, she was able to blot out some of the darkness at home.

My mother never remarried, and when she was fifty-five she went back to school at the University of Colorado and became Mississippi's first school nurse practitioner. She visited local schools on her rounds, taking care of thousands of kids through the years, with all their cuts and scrapes and strep throats. She would drive kids all over north Mississippi to get their eyeglasses or to get their teeth fixed. She went above and beyond the call of duty in everything that she did. When she died, she received commendations from the governor and was the first person inducted into the Mississippi School Nurses Hall of Fame.

————

I mention all this because my conflicts with my father were at the center of my own struggle to know myself—and to be honest with myself and others. This goes to the heart of my mirror moments.

I wasn't like most of the other kids in Amory. I didn't want to grow up to be a doctor, a lawyer, or a teacher. I wanted to be in show business, and I didn't think that living in northeast Mississippi should stop me. *The Beverly Hillbillies* series on CBS made Beverly Hills and Southern California look like Heaven to me, and watching fellow Mississippian Elvis Presley's success in the movies inspired me to go after the same thing.

When I told my mother what I wanted to do, she said, "If you want it, I know you'll figure out how to get it." I knew she would help me in any way she could.

But my father was different. He didn't get involved with my plans for myself, other than to tell me what *his* plans were for me. He desperately wanted me to succeed but according to *his* standards, which meant becoming a doctor.

As he had with the Cheer Man, my father called my show business aspirations a pipe dream. He thought it ridiculous that "this brilliant, outstanding kid wants to waste his life" on what he called my "song-and-dance routine." In high school and college I was in all the plays and musicals, usually in the lead role. I couldn't dance, but I sang and I acted. Still, he never came to a show, only to sporting events.

I think that part of the reason was his family history. His first cousin had been a beautiful actress and high-fashion model named Anita Colby. In the 1930s and 1940s she was known in Hollywood as "The Face." Her photos appeared on the covers of many national magazines, including *Time*. But she never landed a starring film role; instead, she was always the pretty girl who had a couple of scenes. When her looks began to fade, she had a tough time finding work. Eventually Anita gave up acting and modeling and traded her dream for a job as a casting director at Paramount with producer David Selznick, who had won Best Picture Oscars for *Gone with the Wind* and *Rebecca*. Seeing how her career didn't turn out the way she'd wanted it to made my father wary of his son's following Anita down that "yellow brick road."

My father also worried about my habit of wanting the best of everything. For instance, when Johnny Carson came out with his "Carson Collection," I wanted one of his suits. They cost about $150. Most boys got their suits from JCPenney, but my mother took me to The Loft in Tupelo, one of the finest men's stores in northeast Mississippi, and for my fifteenth birthday bought me a Johnny Carson suit. I loved it. I would have rather had that one suit and worn it every Sunday than have a dozen JCPenney suits. This embarrassed my father, because the "uniform" in our town was mostly blue jeans and T-shirts and scuffed-up tennis shoes, and he had a son who was preoccupied with looking sharp. It was all about him, all the time. His little joke was to call me "Mr. Richly."

I'm sure my father—who was a "man's man"—also harbored an unspoken phobia about what my "song-and-dance routine" and my love of style might imply about me. But since I always enjoyed the company of girls, I don't think he worried all *that* much. Instead, I believe he was concerned that I wouldn't fit into a man's world, and that I wouldn't fulfill *his* dream and become a doctor. Ironically, that's what his father had wanted for him. My father had rebelled and become successful on his own, but somehow that didn't stop him from planning out *my* life.

Despite all this, with my mother's support I kept going in the direction that I had discovered pleased me. My father pushed back. I still hadn't told him that I dreaded becoming a doctor, so he wanted me to attend Emory University in Atlanta because it had a fine medical school.

I wanted to attend "Ole Miss"—the University of Mississippi, the land of Archie Manning and Miss Americas.

Emory was closer to Pensacola, where my father lived with "the other woman," who had recently become his new wife. To please him, I applied there, and during my high school senior year the two of us flew to Atlanta, rented a car, and drove to the university for my interviews. After he gave me this whole speech about why I should go through Emory's medical school program, we arrived at the admissions office. He saw a school yearbook on the coffee table, opened it, and saw a picture of a wild-haired kid doing a double flip-off at the camera.

The early 1970s was still a radical time, and Emory was probably more liberal than my father expected. "Oh my God!" he said as he slammed the book shut. He was just furious.

Then the college had "the nerve," in the words of my father, to wait-list me.

What he did next surprised me—and, I have to admit, made me proud of him. He called the head of admissions and, referring to the offensive yearbook picture, said, "How is it possible that my kid, who's president of his high school class, gets straight As, and is one of the stars of the football team and an Eagle Scout, can't get into Emory, and a kid like *that* can?"

Next thing I knew I was accepted at Emory.

I still didn't want to go, but I felt so much guilt over all the trouble my father had gone through to get me in that I couldn't bring myself to look in the mirror, and I waited until the last minute to tell him I'd be going to Ole Miss instead.

My father went crazy. "All my friends are there," I said. To placate him, I promised I'd rush the Sigma Chi fraternity, because he'd been a Sigma Chi at the University of Cincinnati. I also agreed to study premed. He decided to make the best of the situation.

As I'd expected, premed made me miserable, but I stuck with it—not so much because of my father, but because my mother was a nurse and, although she would never insist, I knew that my becoming a doctor would make *her* happy as well. That gave me half a reason to persevere, but I didn't tell her how I really felt because inside I knew that she would have told me to make *myself* happy.

She would have been correct. At Ole Miss, I still longed to be in the plays and produce shows for the campus television station. Looking for something to buoy my spirits at the beginning of my sophomore year, I decided, The heck with it: I'm going to audition for one of the campus musicals. My roommate and Sigma Chi fraternity brother, Dennis Legate, said, "Yeah, but what if you get a part? How are you going to balance that with premed?"

"If I get lucky enough to be cast, I'll just do both," I said.

"Got it," he said. "But what are you going to do about your father?"

Good question.

I tried out, got a call-back, and was cast as the male lead in the Harvey Schmidt–Tom Jones musical *I Do! I Do!* I was also asked to join the University Concert Singers.

Then, one day during rehearsals, the musical's director asked me to consider changing my major. I wanted to; it felt right. But how could I bear more conflict with my father? I talked to my girlfriend at the time, as well as my good friend Marsha Hull and my mother. They all told me to go for it.

But several of my fraternity brothers, also on the premed

track, told me they thought switching majors would be a mistake. And I knew that several people in Amory would have agreed. So many people were counting on me to succeed, and I just couldn't let them down.

I needed to take a long, long look in the mirror and examine my heart.

As usual, my first reaction was to try and find a way to please everyone else and put myself at the end of the line. I didn't want to embarrass my parents. But I realized that not acting on what I knew in my heart, and trying to please everyone else, would doom me to failure in both premed *and* theater and music.

So I finally did what I wanted to do: I changed my major.

I told my dad on the phone. He flipped out. He cussed at me. He said, "I can't believe you're going to embarrass me and your-self. You're out of your mind. Is this your mother's idea?" (At this point he was blaming just about everything he didn't like about me on her.)

"No," I said. That was the truth.

I had expected his reaction, but not the rest of what he said. "If you're going down the 'song-and-dance' road, then you're pay-ing for it yourself," he growled.

I was nineteen years old.

I never got another penny from my father. Instead, I coached and taught swimming at the Amory Municipal Pool, and I used the five thousand dollars or so I made every summer to pay for tuition, books, fraternity dues, clothes, and everything else. I loved that job, and even more than the job I loved that I'd re-spected myself enough to be who I knew I had to be. I was afraid, yes. My father thought I would fail. I wanted to prove I wouldn't. Had I respected him more, I might have listened to him and ended up a frustrated pediatrician in Amory. But that never happened, because the lesson is that if we can connect with what we really want, we can turn off the voices that invariably make us second-guess our choices, and move ahead with our lives under our own control.

————

Just as my mother encouraged me to be true to myself, I also had to learn to let other people choose to be true to themselves. You'd think that after all I'd been through with my father, I might already have figured out that part of the equation. You'd be wrong.

At the start of my senior year at Ole Miss, I was sitting on the steps of College Hill Presbyterian Church in Oxford, Mississippi, with my fraternity brothers, checking out all the new sorority pledges, when I saw a stunning girl walk by. Her name was Mary Donnelly. She was a freshman from Beaumont, Texas, who'd pledged Chi Omega sorority. My friends Anna Katherine Clark and Susan Noble introduced us. Coincidentally, in addition to being in music theory class together, we had both auditioned and subsequently been asked to join the University Song and Dance troupe—known as "The Group"—which traveled around the Southeast as part of the university's recruitment program. We did musical numbers and made speeches about Ole Miss. We sang at inaugurations and conventions. Mary had an incredible voice.

Mary really seemed to know who she was. Her sense of self-possession was irresistible. I asked her to the Ole Miss football game on September 17, 1976, for our first date. After that weekend, I called my mother and said, "I've met the girl I'm going to marry."

We did, in 1982.

I had made this vow even though I'd once told my mother—in my typical grand fashion—that I was determined to marry a Miss Mississippi. Fortunately, my mother was happy for me and didn't remind me of that old promise.

I had, however, always loved beauty pageants. They made ordinary girls into American princesses. I had attended the Miss Mississippi Pageant for the first time when I was fifteen because my good friend Frank Page's sister, Sara, was Miss Amory. My mother drove me and my buddy Mike Burgess to Vicksburg to hang out with Frank and cheer Sara on. By the time I was a high school senior, I had called the pageant's producer, Don Barnes, and talked my way into the Miss Mississippi chorus; I would sing backup in the pageant production over the next several summers.

That's where I met Pat and Briggs Hopson, who ran the Miss Mississippi Pageant, and Bill and Sara Foster, who ran the local Miss Mississippi State University Pageant. In September 1974, I was invited by the Fosters to attend the Miss America Pageant in Atlantic City with them, as a Mississippi delegate. Two future clients were competing at Miss America that year: writer/producer Pam Long as Miss Alabama, and actress Delta Burke as Miss Florida. All of that prepared me for a three-year run directing the Miss University of Mississippi Pageant at Ole Miss while I was a student there. It was a tough job, but *someone* had to go to all the fraternities and sororities and dormitories and get them to put up beautiful and talented girls to compete. I had become the Bert Parks of the Ole Miss campus!

The first year I directed the Miss University Pageant, the winner, Becky Moore from Memphis, was second-runner-up to Miss Mississippi, and the second year I directed it, the winner, Nancy White from Gulfport, was first-runner-up to Miss Mississippi.

When the Miss University Pageant rolled around during my senior year, I recruited Ole Miss coeds who had been runners-up in their home-state pageants the summer before. It was my final year to direct the Ole Miss Pageant, and I was determined that Miss University *had* to win Miss Mississippi. Mary and I had been dating for five months, so I told her, "I'm going to be completely buried in this the entire month of January and most of February." Then, just thinking aloud, I said, "You oughta enter." Mary was beautiful and had a great voice. I figured she'd get in the top ten and it would help make her freshman year memorable. Her Chi Omega sisters agreed.

To my great surprise, and beating all odds, Mary Donnelly won the title of Miss University of Mississippi 1977.

Then she won Miss Mississippi and was on her way to the Miss America Pageant in Atlantic City. And *this* Miss Mississippi was *my* Miss Mississippi.

That's when I started to worry. Not about myself—about Mary. She was still an eighteen-year-old, non-pageant-type girl from Texas who usually wore a ponytail, cowboy boots, and jeans. Though she was completely at ease with who she was, I became obsessed with making her fit the pageant mold. With Miss America in our sights, I was very determined to help the Hopsons transform her into a winner. I wanted to make sure she did everything right, and set out to replace the Mary I knew and loved with my vision of who she had to be.

Instead of learning from how my father treated me, I'd forgotten that while it's okay to be an example to others, you have no business trying to *make* them into what you want them to be. One evening Mary wasn't wearing makeup when I picked her up for a date. I said, "You can't come out here with no makeup on. You're Miss Mississippi!" I patiently lectured her that people would judge her for not being who they expected her to be.

Mary would have none of it. She didn't want to tease her hair and use all that makeup just to go out to Captain D's or Pizza Hut. And she let me know in no uncertain terms that while she appreciated my concern, she could take care of herself. Luckily, my ears were open. I promised to do better. Miss Ohio won the Miss America title that year, and I'm still not over it!

After the Miss America pageant, Mary entered Sigma Chi

Derby Day as one of her Chi Omega sorority's representatives. In one contest, she and another girl sat on a greased log over a mud pit. They'd hit each other with pillows until one of them fell in. Mary was winning, then suddenly got knocked off the log—and came up completely covered in mud. Afterward, a bitchy pageant girl from Memphis walked up to Mary and with great disdain said, "So, *this* is Miss Mississippi?"

This time, Mary and I both laughed. If Mary was willing to fall in the mud for a good cause—which I thought was cool—or to go out not looking like "Miss Mississippi," it was her own business. And it was a good reminder for me that not only did I have to pay attention to liking myself, but I had to be open to and not interfere with others.

———

Life presents all sorts of opportunities for us to look in the mirror and realize who we are and who we want to be. For me, these moments often involve Mary.

Mary became—in addition to a parent deeply involved with all aspects of raising our children—a successful actress and Christian recording artist. I couldn't be more proud of her, and I take great pleasure in every one of her successes. When she shines, I get to shine. But on one occasion I suffered from such a bout of pridefulness that it took Mary's teaching me a lesson in humility through the example of her own strong character to help me see my mistake. This lesson came just recently into our lives, but it is important to share it here now.

Mary was booked to sing in a Christmas concert at the Gertrude Ford Center for the Performing Arts at Ole Miss in December of 2007. She would be joined by Christian artist Steve Amerson and an old college friend, Broadway's Laurie Gayle Stephenson. I did everything in my power to make sure the concert would be a sellout, and, because of how much I loved her and how proud I was of her talents, I wanted to make sure that Mary would be perceived as the star. I wanted Mary's musical moments to be the highlight of the evening, and indeed, the concert sold out in no small part because she was considered the main attraction.

Everything went as planned until the morning of the concert. Mary awoke with a tickle in her throat, and she said words to me that I'd never before heard her say during our thirty-two years together: "Love, I'm in trouble." By mid-morning she had a full-blown flu. And despite her doctor's care, she had almost completely lost her voice.

I was devastated, and while I prayed for a miracle, I began to feel that somehow I was being punished for wanting her to be the star. Everything I'd done that year, from my charity work to all the rest, I believed I'd done for others—and I had decided, while taking pride in my work, that Mary's show was the only thing I considered my personal reward. I'm talking about something that really made *me* happy. And I took it for granted that I would be rewarded. Everything had worked beautifully in the preparation. How ironic that the one thing I never considered was that the star might not be able to perform.

By concert time, after a lengthy discussion with Ford Center director Norm Easterbrook, I thought Mary should tell the audience how sick she was and simply turn the concert over to Steve and Laurie and back out. But Mary had a different plan. "We've always told the children that Haskells aren't quitters," she said, sitting in her dressing room. "Well, I have to try. Help me with my gown!"

Mary mustered her courage, walked onstage, and made it through the first trio with Steve and Laurie. Then she kept the microphone and told the audience of twelve hundred that she had not been this sick in thirty years, but an Ole Miss Rebel doesn't go down easily. The crowd cheered as Mary told them she wanted to keep going. "I'm going to try," she said, when they finally settled down. "That which doesn't kill us will serve to make us stronger."

After the concert I had to meet hundreds of people, all of whom said Mary had been fabulous. Every time I said, "We're so heartbroken that she couldn't sing," the response was—and this is the part that's so amazing—"We all know she can sing. But the strength and courage she showed is the most incredible thing we've ever seen." I knew they wanted to make Mary feel better, and we appreciated their support; she was so gracious, accepting, and beautiful. But I remained devastated—and I didn't understand why. If what had happened was all right with Mary, why couldn't I get over it too?

After the show we held a dinner for about twenty people. Mary served as hostess. She couldn't say a word but she was incredible. At one point she grabbed my hand and whispered, "One day it will all be revealed. One day we'll know. My lesson in this is humility. Maybe the lesson was to show us that even though we always try to do good, we're not immune to the things that happen to others; we won't *always* get the result we expect. I lost my voice. But maybe the purpose was to show that even in the worst possible situation, we can come through it. And maybe it's a lesson in humility for you, too," she said.

Mary was right. There's nothing wrong with hurting when a loved one is hurt, but the concert—although I thought it was all about her—had become all about me.

Back in Los Angeles I went to see my pastor at Bel Air Presbyterian Church, Reverend Carolyn "Care" Crawford, as I often did when I needed counsel.

"Was I being punished for being prideful?" I asked.

"No, Sam. God isn't like that."

"Then why did this happen? Is it because I put too much emphasis on Mary? Too much emphasis on this being the most important thing in our lives instead of God?"

"No, there's something else."

Later I figured out what she meant.

The lesson is that the concert was never about me. Mary was right; I had to be more humble. The concert was about *everyone* there, from the performers to the audience. Just because I'd been disappointed didn't mean the show had been a failure.

Far from it. The Tupelo paper did a big review of the concert the next day and said that one of the most impressive things about this wonderful event was Mary Haskell's courage, strength, and character.

Of course. Mary has always been my shining example, and in that moment onstage she taught me the importance of not losing sight of what really matters. She showed me that God can definitely provide a lesson for us amidst what appears to be utter disappointment.

———

When we come to a crossroads where we face a choice between right and wrong, we may sometimes be confused about which is which. But if we have a good grip on who we are, and know that we like who we are, we'll always be able to come back to the "path of truth." It's when we forget who we are that we have a hard time getting back to the path we've created for ourselves. Once I graduated from Ole Miss, my education in being honest with myself and others was about to be tested.

I knew in my heart that the next step on the path I'd created for myself would have to take me to Los Angeles, California. I definitely wanted a show business career, but when I was faced with the challenge of actually leaving Amory and pursuing my plans, a little voice on my shoulder kept whispering that throwing all my chips into the show business pot seemed too presumptuous, too impulsive. So I came up with a solid reason to go all the way to the West Coast that would not only give me something to fall back on, but would keep me from being judged by those I'd left behind. Law school. I'd taken my LSATs and had been accepted at Southwestern School of Law. I was hardly keen on law, but the idea of failing in show business and going back to "Mayberry" with my tail between my legs—and proving my father and the other naysayers correct—terrified me. At worst, I rationalized, entertainment law was still *entertainment*.

On my first day in class a professor gave one of those "Look around the room—half of you won't be here next year" speeches. My heart jumped and I instantly realized that if I only had the courage, I'd be among the missing. Two days later, after still not finding an apartment, I sat in my dreary room at the Best Western Motel in downtown Los Angeles, and I burst into tears. It was the same old dilemma all over again. I kept second-guessing myself: What was I doing? Was it all just a dream? Why did I think I could make it? Why did I need to make it here instead of at home? I had been offered jobs at a couple of TV stations back in Mississippi for $35,000 a year—a lot of money then. I missed Mary, who was still at Ole Miss, and I missed my family.

I called my mother. She said, "Then just pack up and come back."

I called Mary. She was compassionate, but would have none of my defeatist attitude. Instead, she challenged me. "As long as I've known you," which had been two years, "all you've talked about is California. You cannot come back here without giving it a chance. You cannot."

I called my mother again. "Mary's talked some sense into me. I'm going to stay and try to stick this out." For the first time, someone else's opinion trumped my mother's. Mary was emerging as the greater influence.

I had to do *something* that would lead me in the right direction, and I needed someone willing to help me find a reason for hanging in there.

I went to the placement office at Southwestern and said, "I need to know the names of some prominent attorneys who've graduated from here." I'd decided to set up informational interviews in order to make contacts and perhaps secure an internship or future position. I learned that Los Angeles mayor Tom Bradley was an alumnus, as were several big-name movie studio people. Also, Ruth Engelhardt, the senior vice president of business affairs at the William Morris Agency, had graduated from the school.

I knew the agency's name because I'd read about it in Garson Kanin's book *Hollywood*.

I called Ruth immediately. Her assistant, Laura Moreno, laughed gently the first time I asked to come in. "You must be kidding. Ruth Engelhardt's one of the most important people in this business. You can't just meet with her."

Still, I kept calling every week and talking to Laura. I think she began to melt a little bit, but she still wouldn't put me through or make an appointment for me. Then, on the Friday before Labor Day in 1978—a lucky day for me, I think, since the Cheer Man also came the Friday before Labor Day—I made my usual call to Ruth's office, and this time she answered her own phone: "This is Ruth Engelhardt."

I almost stopped breathing. "Ms. Engelhardt," I finally said, "this is Sam Haskell. I've been calling your office every week for two months trying to get a meeting with you. I know how busy you are, but if you could find five minutes to meet me I'd be so grateful. I'm a student at Southwestern Law and I want to learn more about what you do."

To my surprise, she said, "Okay. I want to meet the face that goes with this voice."

My Southern accent was much thicker at that time.

"Can you come today?" she asked. "Now?" I drove straight to Beverly Hills.

Ruth spent three hours with me that afternoon. She told me about her life, about Southwestern, about her career, about William Morris. I told her that I knew about the William Morris Agency because Johnny Carson talked about it all the time. She laughed. I said, "I also read Garson Kanin's book *Hollywood* when I was sixteen."

Of course she'd read the book, but she let me go on as I told her the story of MGM chief Louis B. Mayer's allowing only one agent on the back lot during the '30s and '40s—Abe Lastfogel, head of William Morris, because he admired his character and integrity.

Ruth asked about my aspirations, dreams, and goals. I told her that I'd been involved in several concerts at Ole Miss and had produced a couple of plays and closed-circuit television shows. I'd also been a performer. I think Ruth realized immediately that I understood actors, producers, writers, and directors—which I did, although only in the microcosm of college life. But she could tell that I knew what I was talking about.

"Have you ever thought about being an agent?" she asked.

"What does an agent do?"

Ruth told me that agents basically get work for the agency's clients. "To begin with, young agents work with the clients of senior agents, and as your relationships and experiences grow, you can start to sign your own clients," she explained. "The agency generally charges ten percent of the fee for every job we get for our clients."

I sat there nodding my head, taking it all in.

"We also package many of the television shows that you grew

up watching," she continued, "like *The Dick Van Dyke Show, The Danny Thomas Show, The Andy Griffith Show,* and *Bat Masterson.*"

"What does 'package' mean?" I asked.

"It's complicated," she said, "but basically we have a group of agents who put the series idea, the writers and producers, and the talent together, and then sell that package to the network. The agency gets a sales fee for every William Morris–packaged series a network puts on the air."

I didn't know the ins and outs of the business side yet, but I knew I could learn it. Just the idea of working with actors and actresses and writers whom I loved sold me. I knew that I had come to the right place. I thought, *This* is what I want to do. "How do I start?" I asked.

"First of all, dismiss the whole idea of law school. And you'll need to start in the mailroom."

"What's that?"

"You do all the chores and run errands for each of the agents. You deliver mail, of course. You learn the business from the ground floor up."

That interested me. The mailroom seemed like a challenge that would help me create the opportunities and relationships I'd need in order to take the next step toward my goal. And I was absolutely relieved that I didn't have to stay in law school.

"The mailroom doesn't pay much," Ruth added, watching for my reaction, "but some of the most important people in this business started there. I think you've got what it takes. And by the way, some people who come into the mailroom *already* have law and accounting degrees. And they still have to spend two to three years there before they can become an agent. You're twenty-three; you could be an agent by the time you're twenty-six."

My mouth probably hung open. Then she asked, "Do you

play softball?" I thought for a second about how my father had to push me onto the baseball diamond as a kid. "Yes," I said.

"Great, we need new people on our softball team, too."

I applied to the agent training program that day. Afterward, I realized that for three glorious hours, I'd felt like my old self again. I wasn't onstage, but I was in the heart of Hollywood. I didn't wonder for a second if I'd made the right decision. I didn't check with anyone before changing course. I realized that I had found the common ground for the common good, while not losing who I was or what I wanted in the process.

I guess if you have to repeat a lesson and remember a promise to be true to yourself often enough, eventually you get it.

FOUR

Give What They Want to Get What You Want

Think about what you want, think about who can help you get it, and think about how to make them happy about giving it to you.

—MARY KIRKPATRICK HASKELL

My mother believed that while everyone should be responsible for pursuing their own dreams, it was cocky to think you could always do it completely on your own. Not only was it perfectly okay to have help, it was preferable, especially if you could find a way to make others truly happy to lend a hand in the true spirit of sharing. Her way was to give others what they wanted in order to get what she wanted. (You can also give what *you* want to get what you want. If you want respect, give respect. If you want love, give love. If you need help, give help.)

My mother was a long-standing member of the Fidelia Ladies' Club in Amory and part of the big Christmas Parade Float Committee. The club was very proud of its creations and had won the grand prize for best float several years in a row. Putting these projects together was a big job, and most of the work and organization fell on the chairman: coming up with a theme, designing the float, purchasing the materials, deciding which children ride the float as characters supporting the theme— always a big deal—and then actually building the float.

When my mother became chairman, she decided to ask the entire club, and not just the float committee, for help. That year, Santa's Workshop was the theme, and knowing that every parent coveted a seat on the float for their kids, she announced that the children of every parent who helped design or build the float would get to ride down Main Street as Santa's elves. In other words, in exchange for help, she'd help them in return. Very quickly she had more volunteers than she needed.

Of course, the Fidelia Club won first place again, and I got to be one of the elves!

———

Each of us has our own goals and dreams, and our own visions of what we want to achieve in life. No one else can provide that for us. The question, though, is how do we make those dreams come true? How do we get there? Library shelves are stuffed with books containing "surefire" strategies and suggestions. But because of my mother's encouragement and wise example, the question for me has never just been about how to get what I want, but how to create an atmosphere in which others are genuinely happy to help because we can all be rewarded in the end.

During my twenty-five years at William Morris, as I rose through the ranks from the mailroom, I refined this idea and created a concept I call being "thoughtfully political." I've lectured on it around the country, from boardrooms to churches to school assemblies. The response has always been enthusiastic. Afterward, people always want to know how to best apply the concept to their own lives. I realize that some people might focus on the word "political" as a negative, as if being conscious of what you want and figuring out how to get it means doing something dishonest. Not at all. Being political is simply having a thorough sense of the big picture so you can see the people and issues involved in three dimensions, including the other people's points of view.

And to me, "thoughtfully" has always been the more important word. To be thoughtful means to "think" about what you want. If you're thoughtful, you understand that we are all related, and that to achieve a positive outcome for everyone involved, there's an absolute need for give-and-take. Being thoughtfully political is simply a way of overcoming natural obstacles to the integration of your needs and the needs of others. It's a way of figuring out where the common ground for the common good lies, while not losing who you are or what you want in the process.

The key is to treat others as you would like to be treated.

It's the Golden Rule.

———

Even with Ruth Engelhardt's endorsement, from the moment I started interviewing for the William Morris training program, I had to focus on finding a way to get hired, and then to please each of the many agents who grilled me during two weeks of interviews, so they would push me to the next level instead of showing me the door. And I had to do it honestly—not by pretending to be what I thought they wanted, but by being my authentic self, Southern accent and all.

When I finally met with William Morris's chief operating officer, Walt Zifkin, I had learned he would make the decision about whether or not I'd get the chance to work sixteen hours a day as an agent trainee earning almost nothing to learn the business.

Mr. Zifkin looked me over quietly from head to toe. "I've been getting all these reports on what a nice kid you are," he said. That made me breathe a bit more easily. "But you're actually too tall to be an agent." Hmm. There *were* a lot of short people in the office. "Don't you think this is going to be a culture shock for you?" he continued. Now I began to understand what he was getting at. "You're this tall, white-bread, gentile kid from Mississippi, coming to Los Angeles to work for a primarily Jewish company, in a primarily Jewish, liberal business."

Then he posed *the* question. "Why do you think you're going to fit in?"

I realized I couldn't be defensive or simply cite my enthusiasm and qualifications. I had to create a way into the job by making him happy to help me, and to do it honestly. Again, the solution was to be myself. If I was so different, I had to turn that to my advantage.

On impulse, I told him a story about my mother.

"I was raised in a Southern Baptist church in Amory, Mississippi. We had a fire-and-brimstone preacher who, every Sunday, said, 'You're going to Hell if you don't believe in the Lord Jesus Christ as the Messiah born to save you from your sins,' and all that sort of thing you see on the televangelical shows.

"One Sunday, when I was nine years old, I came home from church and, over lunch, asked my deeply spiritual and religious mother a question.

" 'Momma, why is it that [let's call him] Mr. Smith, who sits in the front row of the church every Sunday, who is mean to his children and gets drunk and does all these terrible things, but proclaims he is a Christian—why is he going to Heaven? And Mrs. Siegel and Mr. Rubenstein, who open their stores on Christmas Eve and give all the poor black children coats and shoes—why are they going to Hell?'

"My mom thought for a minute. 'You're right,' she said. 'We

are all called to live godly lives, and Mrs. Siegel and Mr. Ruben-stein are excellent examples.' "

By not losing my cool, I had let Mr. Zifkin know that I em-braced all faiths and would have no difficulty adjusting. I am a Christian. But I don't believe that other people are wrong for not being Christian, or that they should be punished for believing something other than what I do. Faith is a very personal matter, and we all believe in the faith our parents taught us, and their parents taught them, until we reach an age when we determine our own beliefs.

With that answer, I showed Mr. Zifkin that I thought well on my feet in an awkward and challenging situation and that I could be both persuasive *and* truthful. I also let him know that I could thrive in an unfamiliar environment.

The truth is that Mr. Zifkin liked me and *wanted* to find a rea-son to hire me if I could help him overcome his fear that I might not only be uncomfortable myself, but make others feel awk-ward. I gave him what he needed—confidence in me—and got what I wanted: a job. He hired me on the spot.

By the way, it took six years, but Mr. Zifkin finally let me know that he'd become very happy with his decision to bring me into William Morris. "I almost didn't hire you that day," he con-fided in me over lunch. "But after you told me that story, I real-ized I had to give you a try. Now, I realize what a mistake it would have been not to have hired you." For me, that was the compli-ment of all time.

———

Several years later I met a charming young man from Louisiana named Bryan Lourd. He was roommates at USC with the son of a client and friend, producer Bob Precht. After graduation, Bryan decided he wanted to be an agent and Bob introduced us, hop-ing I'd be the perfect person to mentor Bryan because he, too,

was a gentile from a small Southern town, and would have to figure out if he was comfortable in the Beverly Hills show business
culture. For me, the benefits were obvious: It would be great to
have someone in the business with a background to which I
could relate. To gain that friendship, I gave Bryan what he
needed: frank talk about the challenges he would face and encouragement to give it a try. Because of how my mother raised
me, my support was instinctive, not premeditated. He, in turn,
needed someone with experience to support him. After we
spoke, Bryan thought he could handle it. I helped him get into
the William Morris training program, and he quickly became an
agent.

Eventually, Bryan left William Morris and became a top agent
at the Creative Artists Agency (CAA)—our competition—an
agency founded by former William Morris agent Mike Ovitz.
Though it was sad to see him go, it was the right move and I
wished him well. A few years later, Ovitz and the other founding
partners left CAA, and after creating a name for himself as well
as a power base with clients like Meryl Streep, Bryan became
one of the new partners. Two Southern men had treated each
other as they wanted to be treated and were on their way to success in Hollywood.

These days, even though Bryan is one of the most powerful
people in Hollywood, and I am no longer at William Morris,
we're still good friends based on those first encounters, plus
years of working together afterward. In fact, the day I left
William Morris in 2004, Bryan was one of the very first to call,
asking if he could help me make my next move. That loyalty
meant more to me than he will ever know.

———

My encounters with three actresses at different times in my career demonstrates how my mother's advice—to give what others

need in order to get what you need—works, no matter what the era.

I'd always fantasized about meeting the stars. When I was ten, I shelved books at the Amory Public Library and took every opportunity to read each book, magazine, or newspaper I could find to learn about Hollywood. We had material on all of the top Hollywood stars: Clark Gable, Loretta Young, James Stewart, Elizabeth Taylor, Grace Kelly, Judy Garland, Vivien Leigh, Katharine Hepburn, Humphrey Bogart, and Bette Davis, and I read them *all*.

Bette Davis, in particular, fascinated me. Somehow, she didn't seem like a typical movie star. She was more handsome than beautiful, and she seemed so grounded. I just loved her. My fascination never faded, even as I grew older. I was dying to meet her someday.

In the spring of 1982, after I'd been an agent for two years, I was responsible for covering every single talk show and variety show on television; if there was a spot into which I could book a William Morris client, it was my job to find it. I got hundreds of William Morris clients on the air, and I was excited to go to the office every day.

I also worked with the producers and packagers we represented, to help them put together their network television projects. Sir David Frost (and his partners) had come up with a two-hour special called *The American Movie Awards*. We sold it to Brandon Tartikoff at NBC as an alternative to ABC's yearly Academy Awards telecast.

Deborah Miller assigned me to the new David Frost special, and I was thrilled to be a part of its creation.

At the first production meeting Sir David announced that producer Hal Wallis would get the first *American Movie Awards* Lifetime Achievement Award. Wallis had produced so many movies I can't list them all here. But they included *Anne of the*

Thousand Days, Barefoot in the Park, The Man Who Came to Dinner, The Maltese Falcon, and *Casablanca.*

Mr. Frost said he wanted Bette Davis to present the award. She and Wallis had done several movies together, including *Jezebel,* for which Miss Davis had won her second Best Actress Oscar, in 1938.

"Who knows Bette Davis?" he asked, explaining that *someone* had to call and ask if she'd appear.

The room, full of producers, writers, and network executives, remained silent.

"All right, does anyone know Marion Rosenberg, Bette Davis's agent?"

I didn't know Marion, but I raised my hand and said, "I'll call her." Mr. Frost said, "Thank you, Sam, but Marion will probably make you call Bette yourself. She's . . . tough. Do you think you're up for the job?"

I'd barely replied, "Yes sir," when the older men in the room started telling me horror stories about Bette Davis, suggesting that I should reconsider having volunteered. I didn't care what they thought of her, I was determined to talk to Bette Davis.

Sir David told me to call the next morning and then report back to him.

At 9 A.M. sharp I called Marion Rosenberg. As predicted, she told me I'd have to call Miss Davis directly. She warned me that there would be many questions and that the way I answered those questions would determine the outcome.

When I got through to Miss Davis's assistant, Kathryn Sermak, she put me on hold. It seemed like I waited a half hour, but it was probably only five minutes. While on hold, I prayed that God would help me find the right words. My prayer was interrupted by a voice I knew all too well. "Mr. Haskell, this is Bette Davis. . . . What exactly would you have me do, and how does this involve Mr. Hal Wallis?"

I explained—it probably sounded like a rehearsed speech, but it came straight from my heart—why we were honoring Hal Wallis, and why she was the best-qualified person to give him the Lifetime Achievement Award.

"What exactly are *The American Movie Awards*?" she asked.

I explained the idea behind Sir David's show.

She laughed and said, "David will have his hands full with the Academy over this one!" That led into a fifteen-minute discussion about who I was, my age, where my accent came from, how long I had been an agent, etc. I must have answered all of the questions correctly, because Miss Davis agreed to do the show.

I thanked her. No, I gushed; I admit it. I was about to hang up when she said, "Mr. Haskell, there is one condition. I want you standing on the red carpet when I arrive, you'll walk me into the theater, and stay in the Green Room with me until it's time for me to present Mr. Wallis his award."

She didn't have to ask me twice. To get what she said she wanted—"the company of this funny young agent with the heavy Southern accent, who was both earnest and eager" (I guess I was somehow different from other people who had made business calls to her)—she ultimately gave me what I wanted as well: her presence at the awards ceremony.

Naturally, David Frost was overjoyed, and he told everyone at NBC and William Morris how "the kid called Bette Davis and convinced her to be on the show."

Roger Moore hosted the show, and my client, Debbie Allen, along with the cast of the TV show *Fame* danced down Hollywood Boulevard, then burst into the theater to complete their production number. Dudley Moore, Debbie Reynolds, Jane Fonda, Liza Minnelli, and Ginger Rogers were all there as well. David Frost was thrilled. It was a great moment for me. I'd proven myself to my clients, and somehow made Ms. Davis happy to help me.

A month later I got an invitation to Bette Davis's seventy-fourth birthday party.

The party started at 7 P.M. at Miss Davis's penthouse apartment on Havenhurst Drive in Hollywood. I arrived at 6:45, and I drove around the block until 6:55. Then I parked, rode the elevator up, and rang the doorbell. Miss Davis answered the door herself. "Well, Mr. Haskell," she said, "how perfectly prompt you are."

She asked me in, and then turned to her assistant Kathryn and said, "That will be ten dollars!" Playing off my quizzical look, she explained, "I bet Kathryn ten dollars that YOU would be the first to arrive."

Miss Davis took me on a tour of her beautifully appointed apartment. Everyone else arrived "fashionably late," which meant that I had the hostess all to myself for half an hour. In her living room, Miss Davis showed me a portrait of herself that hung over the mantel. It had been fashioned after her character Margo Channing in the Academy Award-winning film, *All About Eve*. "Now *that's* the way I want to be remembered," she said.

She also showed me both of her Oscars, displayed prominently in her den, and we discussed her disappointment at not being cast to play Scarlett O'Hara in *Gone with the Wind*. I couldn't believe *she* was telling these things to *me*. It was incredible.

When Mary and I married the following December, Miss Davis sent us a congratulatory note, and I realized yet again how wrong my father and others had been to think I had thrown my life away by coming to Hollywood. I was so happy—both to be making good impressions and to be befriending the Hollywood stars of my childhood fantasies.

———

The second of these three women made me laugh when I met her, and she still makes me laugh today. Debbie Allen, my second client (Kathie Lee Gifford was my first), has always been a great soul mate. I'd wanted to represent Debbie Allen from the moment I was hired at William Morris. She'd had a role in the movie *Fame* and was cast in the TV version that went on the air in January 1982 on NBC. Her William Morris agents worked in our New York office. I told them that she was going to need a television agent on the Coast. "Let me help you," I said. "Let me be your West Coast contact." They agreed because of the way I asked. I'd learned that offering to help by saying "Let me help you" instead of "Let me do this" was a nonthreatening way of opening the door to let myself in. I was confident enough that once I got in the door, I'd stay inside the room.

Debbie and I finally met during the taping of *The NBC Family Christmas,* in December 1981, when the producer, Bob Precht, summoned me. "We've got a problem with Debbie Allen," he said. "She won't sign her contract."

Debbie had probably been a little bit of a diva to one of the production assistants, refusing to come out of her dressing room to do her big number with the cast of *Fame.*

Precht dispatched me to her dressing room, I knocked, and she said to come in.

"Ms. Allen, I'm Sam Haskell."

"And?"

"I'm one of your agents at William Morris."

"Oh, you are? Well, look at this contract! This says I work for scale. I don't work for scale. I just got a Tony nomination for playing Anita in *West Side Story*! I just starred in *Ragtime*! I'm starring in *Fame*! That's why I'm here!"

"Ms. Allen, I know," I said. "You are one of the most important clients we have, and I am honored just to be in your presence. What can I do to make this better?"

She got a big smile on her face. "Baby, if you can go tell Mr. Precht, Mr. Ed Sullivan's son-in-law, that I love my Bob Mackie dress, and get him to agree to give it to me, I'll sign the contract."

"I'll be right back," I told her.

I ran back to Bob Precht. "Here's how to solve this nightmare," I said. "I know you paid ten thousand dollars for this Bob Mackie dress. You own it. But who else besides Debbie Allen will ever wear it? Give it to Debbie Allen and we can get her to sign the contract."

He said, "Give her the damn dress."

I ran back: "Ms. Allen, you can keep the dress."

"I'll sign the contract," she said, "and I want you in my life." We've been friends and business partners ever since!

———

The third actress, Kirstie Alley, was a client for many years. She's very smart, beautiful, and a little eccentric. She has also battled her weight for a long time.

A few years ago, I went to a Pier 1 commercial shoot with her when she was at her largest. She knew the truth, but couldn't face the fact that she'd become so large. One of the PAs had to lace her up in a corset, under her gown, like Mammy lacing Scarlett in *Gone with the Wind*.

After the shoot I had to have one of these "come to Jesus" meetings with her because she had complained to me, "Why can't I get the lead in all of the movies and TV series that I'm interested in? Why can't I be the love interest?"

I looked at her, at her beautiful face, and knew I just had to be honest. "Because you're seventy-five pounds overweight," I said. "You've become a character actress right before our eyes. You are so pretty, but in Hollywood, pretty is thin. You can get supporting parts as a heavy woman, but not roles like the once trim and gorgeous Kirstie Alley everyone knew."

Something clicked in her eyes then. She knew that I loved her, and at that moment, though it wasn't easy, she decided to face the fact that she no longer liked who she was. She needed a way to figure out how to like herself again, to conquer the constant struggle with her weight. How could she turn this weakness to her advantage?

That's how the Showtime series *Fat Actress* was born. I set my client Brenda Hampton (*7th Heaven*) to write and produce it. I even convinced NBC's Jeff Zucker to guest-star in the first episode. I knew Kirstie was unhappy and needed to work, and I needed to make her happy to help herself. So we decided that she should wear her own experience in public. I told her, "Lots of viewers will identify with you. And then if you want to lose weight, we'll go to Slim-Fast, or we'll go to Jenny Craig, and we'll make a deal where you'll be *paid* to lose weight."

Kirstie wanted to feel better about herself. She felt losing weight was the answer. I wanted her to be happy in her own skin, and in turn, as her agent, to have a client who knew what direction we were going in and why. The series *Fat Actress* gave her a "playing ground" to deal with her weight issues, and the deal with Jenny Craig paid her to lose the weight. She dropped seventy pounds, and the next thing I knew she was on *Oprah* in a bikini!

We both got what we wanted, and everyone was happy!

———

I still laugh about the time I had to be both thoughtfully—and frantically—political just to get a show on the air.

In 1987, my ultimate boss, Jerry Katzman, became Worldwide Head of TV at William Morris. With that overall responsibility, he needed someone to replace him as the agency liaison for NBC. Network head Brandon Tartikoff told Katzman, "I want Haskell to replace you."

At the time, Tartikoff was courting Dick Van Dyke (one of

Tartikoff's wife Lily's favorite actors) to be in a new series. He would play a retired CEO of a big company with three daughters, all business tycoons.

William Morris represented Van Dyke, and his agent was Sol Leon.

Tartikoff gave me the spiel on the show, Leon called Van Dyke to discuss the project, and then Leon asked me to join the conversation and handle the meeting. I had never met Dick, so I asked if he and I could get together in the NBC commissary for an hour before the meeting with Tartikoff to talk it through. I always insisted on having premeetings with my clients before going upstairs to any network meeting.

So there I was a couple of days later in the commissary with Dick Van Dyke. I was ready to sell him on the show. But it turned out Dick Van Dyke did not want to do the series. He didn't like the idea, and he began listing reasons why it wasn't right for him. I listened and memorized everything he said. Then I said, "Dick, I really need to go to the bathroom. Excuse me for a minute, I'll be right back."

I ran down the halls and up the back stairs, went to Brandon Tartikoff's office, and told his assistant, "You've got to let me see Brandon before I bring Dick up here. Give me five minutes." She let me pass, and Tartikoff and I went through every one of Dick's concerns. At the end I said, "And would you put Dick on the phone with your wife and let Lily tell him how much she loves him?"

Then I raced back to the commissary, apologized for taking so long, and explained to Dick that I had also run by Business Affairs to check on another deal. I then took him to Tartikoff's office. The first thing Tartikoff said was "Would you please do me the honor of talking to my wife, Lily? She's your biggest fan." So Dick spoke with her on the phone and had the loveliest conversation. He was now in a good mood.

Then Tartikoff pitched the show, but he had fixed every one of Dick's issues. In fact, he'd changed the entire concept to be what the star wanted. Van Dyke signed the contract.

The show didn't make it past the pilot, and I later heard the criticism, "Good grief, look how much trouble you went to just to get a pilot made that never got on the air and made no money." But it wasn't about the money. It was about finding the common good and common ground. Tartikoff made Van Dyke happy to help him, and I'd made Tartikoff happy to help me.

———

My favorite story about being thoughtfully political happened in 1992, when I was thirty-seven years old and had recently established the Mary Kirkpatrick Haskell Scholarship Foundation, in Amory, Mississippi, in memory of my mom. (She'd died of cancer in 1987 and had made me promise to find a way to help young students who needed financial assistance to attend college, just as she'd been helped forty-five years earlier.) The foundation would provide college scholarships for outstanding and deserving young people from Amory and Monroe County who might not have otherwise qualified financially.

Were she alive, my mother would most likely be embarrassed by all the attention that her life, career, and love of children has posthumously brought her through this foundation, which is based on my promise to her to continue in her footsteps, taking care of the less privileged and always remembering to share my blessings. I know that in her own humble way she'd be pleased that we've staged shows that have raised over $4 million to help over five hundred young people in Mississippi get a college education in her honor.

But at the beginning, my goal was more modest: to raise $1 million over ten years, staging concerts in Amory with big stars—primarily my clients, if they were so inclined. By then I was a successful agent and had many friends and connections I could count on to stand up for a worthy cause. The biannual concerts were called "Stars Over Mississippi."

In 1998, I was about to produce my fourth "Stars Over Mississippi" concert. The performers would include singers Pam Tillis and Bryan White as headliners, and stars like Ann-Margret, Tom Arnold, Marilu Henner, Debbie Allen, Mary Ann Mobley, Diahann Carroll, Laurie Stephenson, Gary Collins, Nell Carter, Marilyn McCoo and Billy Davis, Jr., Kathy Ireland, and of course, Mary Haskell. Mississippi lieutenant governor Ronnie Musgrove, Senator Trent Lott, and Representative (and now Senator) Roger Wicker would attend as well.

To pull off any concert like this required an army. My trusted helpers in Amory—Dot Forbus, Ellen Boyd, and Jean Sanders, Mississippi friends who have known me all my life—had, over the years, figured out the best way to mount this tremendous effort. Every time a concert was produced, they supervised over three hundred volunteers, host homes, drivers, the Friday night gala, and the Saturday morning parade. They called themselves the Bitch Patrol—a nickname they'd proudly earned by handling everything with a velvet glove on one hand and a whip in the other. Though they didn't know it at the time, Dot, Ellen, and Jean were practicing the concept of being "thoughtfully political." They knew exactly how to make people happy to give them what they wanted.

That year I was determined to get "Stars" more national attention. The concert series and foundation had been mentioned in an article on me in *People* magazine in June of 1997, but I wanted the foundation to receive even more recognition in order to bring in more sponsors and more money for the scholarships. That meant putting the concert on the air.

I thought the best place was PBS. My friend Mare Mazur ran

programming for KCET in Los Angeles, one of the public broad-casting flagship stations. If they agreed to show "Stars Over Mississippi," I felt sure all the public television stations would follow.

But how could I convince her to do it in a way that would benefit both of us?

I knew that Mare and I shared an interest in England's royal family, and that gave me an idea. Two years earlier, in 1996, I had met His Royal Highness the Prince Edward, the youngest son of Her Majesty Queen Elizabeth II. I had called his office out of the blue after watching a documentary on PBS called *Edward on Edward*. Prince Edward not only hosted the documentary, but produced it through his company, Ardent Productions.

I loved the show, so I dispatched Ben Silverman, currently president of entertainment at NBC. When he worked for me at William Morris, I had relocated Ben to London to find us some new TV formats. (He did. One was *Who Wants to Be a Million-aire,* and he found another with my William Morris partner Mark Itkin, entitled *Big Brother.*) I asked Ben to contact Ardent's head of development and let them know I'd be calling. I didn't get to speak with the Prince, but Ben passed along the message that if His Royal Highness ever wanted to do business in the United States, "Sam's his guy." (I was then West Coast Head of Televi-sion for the agency.)

Then, on a trip to London in 1996, we set up a meeting. Over a four-hour dinner at the Royal Automobile Club (the RAC), we hit it off. Ben Silverman, Greg Lipstone, Mark Itkin, and our boss Jerry Katzman and his wife Carol joined us. Though we all addressed him as "Sir" and "Your Royal Highness," by the end of the evening the Prince said, "Please call me Edward." I knew then that we would work together, and we did!

I told Mare Mazur, "Prince Edward and I have been working

together for two years. If you will give me a two-hour commitment for my charity concert from Mississippi, and let Prince Edward's company produce it, I bet I can get him to host it."

She talked to the head of KCET, and said, "You got it, but he's
got to host."

Next, I approached Prince Edward and told him everything
about the charity foundation, my mother, the scholarships, and
the concert. I said, "And I can get a deal on PBS, our classiest
American network, for Ardent Productions to produce this special if you will host it." He agreed.

In October of 1998, Prince Edward came to Amory, Mississippi, for an entire week of special activities. The Bitch Patrol
was in full swing. This was the first time a member of the British
Royal Family had ever visited the state, and they wanted everything to be spectacular. The Prince's personal driver there, a
lovely young woman whom I had chosen from Amory, had been
well rehearsed in how to address the Prince: either "Good morning, Your Royal Highness" or "Good morning, Sir."

In a nervous moment, she said, "Good morning, Your Royal-
ness." He just laughed, but I was mortified!

As part of the week's schedule, Prince Edward, Mayor
Thomas Griffith, and I planted a magnolia tree in the city park
for the Garden Club. Prince Edward took his cameras all over
town and interviewed people behind the scenes for the show.
Aunt Betty hosted a dinner party in Prince Edward's honor. She
was in a swivet—a Southern expression for turmoil—the entire
week because she wanted everything to be perfect. She needn't
have worried. Aunt Betty served a wonderful Southern meal
while the Prince laughed the entire evening at my uncle Hal's
hysterical stories. The other dinner guests included Mary, my
brother Jamie and his wife, and Erik Sterling and Jason Winters
from Los Angeles.

Amory chef Steve Stockton whipped up a menu fit for a prince. Edward's favorites included the Southern crab cakes, the roasted bacon pecans, the shrimp Charlene in pastry cups, and the baked rum apples stuffed with apricots. My cousin Mary Rogers provided one of the highlights of the evening as she described how Aunt Betty had sent her on a dozen errands to help with the party, including dispatching her to Edna Hill's house in search of an extra sterling meat fork. She even asked the Prince if his mother ever made him run last-minute errands like that. Edward loved my aunt and uncle and cousins. We laughed for three straight hours!

Two days before the Saturday concert, the Prince and I were invited to speak at the Amory Rotary Club. I did a thirty-minute talk about—what else?—being thoughtfully political. I told the audience of 150 that anything was possible if you practiced that principle.

When it was Prince Edward's turn to speak, he thanked everyone for their kind welcome and said how much he had enjoyed experiencing "Southern hospitality." Then he said something I'll never forget: "I've been wondering these past six days *how on earth* I came to be in Amory, Mississippi. And now I've finally figured it out: I've been thoughtfully politicized."

The whole room erupted in laughter. He was right. And everybody was happy.

By Friday, everyone was unhappy. Although the concert's stars were all flying into Memphis and the evening's gala went off without a hitch, around midnight it started to rain—a heavy, gray Mississippi downpour. Two days earlier the Tupelo television station's weatherman had predicted clear skies for the weekend. Anxious, I called the general manager to ask if his weatherman was usually accurate. His reply: "If my weatherman was accurate, I wouldn't be able to afford him!"

That certainly explained the late Friday thunderstorm. But my mother always looked at the glass as half full and never ever gave up believing things would work out positively. So, I figured the rainstorm would blow over by morning.

It didn't. The Saturday parade was scheduled to begin at 9 A.M., but by 6 A.M. the whole family was up, watching the rain. I spoke to the Bitch Patrol hourly, and when the rain began to back off, we decided to go ahead with the parade even if the stars had to hold umbrellas.

Though it rained off and on all afternoon, we managed to squeeze in a dry rehearsal. But the storms returned around 5 P.M. The show was scheduled for 7, and ticket holders arrived with umbrellas open to keep from getting drenched. You could hardly see the stage from the field with all those umbrellas obstructing the view. The crowd was becoming restless. What a mess! I stood in the corner of the Green Room at the Amory National Guard Armory and felt like crying. This was our most important concert yet—televised, hosted by the Prince. I couldn't bear to see it wash away.

At that moment, Ann-Margret walked up, took me by the shoulders, said nothing, looked right into my eyes with the most reassuring smile, hugged me, and went back to her chair next to her husband, Roger Smith. I can imagine that every minister in town was praying for the rain to stop; I know that my pastor in California, Carolyn "Care" Crawford, was, because I'd called her.

Suddenly, at 7 P.M. sharp, the rain stopped. The concert went on as planned. I later discovered that although the skies were clear and the stars shone brightly over Amory, the rest of Monroe County had gotten drenched. I had been blessed by my mother's presence all evening!

When the show was over, the cameras put away, and the last stragglers gone, the rain returned.

———

After the Prince's week in Amory, Mary and I were thrilled to receive an invitation to come to Windsor Castle "to meet someone special." I knew that Edward meant his then-girlfriend, Sophie Rhys-Jones. The Queen had given her blessing to the relationship, and Sophie, who was a publicist in London, was dearly loved by Edward's entire family.

Even though their relationship was common knowledge, I had never talked about Sophie with the Prince. But when he said "someone special," I said, "Is it Sophie Rhys-Jones?"

"I assumed you knew about her," he said, with a curious smile. "But why, all this time, have you never mentioned it?"

"Out of respect."

"I really appreciate that," he said. "That's the reason I think it's time for you to meet her."

Mary and I loved Sophie from the moment we met her during that special weekend at Windsor Castle. The four of us have enjoyed our multiple visits in Los Angeles, Edinburgh, and London more than I can describe. We laugh often and much.

I think it says a lot about the Prince that when he travels to Los Angeles, instead of staying at the Four Seasons or some other posh, expensive hotel, he likes to stay at our home in Encino. Sometimes Sophie is with him, and, occasionally the odd member of his PPO team stays at our house too!

Hmm. Now who's been thoughtfully politicized?

FIVE

No Man Is a Failure
Who Has Friends

My mother's life was the best example of the importance of having special friends. Hers were her sister, Betty Rogers; my high school English teacher, Jeffie Robinson; Virginia Cole; and Helen Rutledge. She could open her heart to these women, know they'd listen, and get emotional support and honest feedback without being judged. And in good times they celebrated together.

My aunt Betty was always my mother's closest friend. She has lived in Amory her whole life, and even now tells me that not a day passes that someone does not confide in her how much they loved her sister. These encounters often happen in the unlikeliest of places. A few years ago, after Aunt Betty had spent a couple of weeks in the hospital, a nurse wheeled her out to my uncle Hal's car. "Did I happen to know you at West Amory?" the nurse asked.

Aunt Betty explained that she had been secretary to the principal of West Amory Elementary School. My mother had been the nurse for all of Amory's schools, and because most illnesses occurred in grade school, she was there often.

The nurse stopped the wheelchair, came around the front, and put her hands on my aunt's shoulders. "You're telling me that Miss Mary was your *sister*?"

"Yes."

"Well, she was the sweetest woman I have ever known. All the folks in West Amory think she's one of the finest women who has ever lived. I wish I had known she was your sister. I would have been in your room every day trying to do something nice for you at this hospital."

Aunt Betty shares stories like this all the time. And I've gotten hundreds and hundreds of letters from parents and kids, now grown, who still think of my mother this way.

———

When I think about friendship I always recall the final fifteen minutes of Frank Capra's movie *It's a Wonderful Life*. After George Bailey (played by Jimmy Stewart) gets to see what life in his hometown of Bedford Falls would have been like had he never been born, he returns to his house and finds it full of people there to help him save the Bailey Building & Loan. Why? He'd helped many of them in *their* hours of crisis. Others are drawn in by the consistency of his character and integrity. And then, to drive the point home, when George opens the copy of *Tom Sawyer* that Angel Second Class Clarence Odbody has left behind, he discovers this written inside: "No man is a failure who has friends."

I couldn't agree more.

When I was little and talking to my mother about my friends, she said, "As you grow older, if you can find five true friends, then you will be lucky."

I did, and I am.

Mary jokes that I have more *best* friends than anyone she's ever known. "You have a best friend in Mississippi, a best friend in Texas, a best friend in Burbank, a best friend at CBS, a best friend from high school, a best friend at church—and I haven't even gotten started."

I call them my "best" friends because it's genuinely how I feel. "Close" somehow doesn't sit right.

Mary points out exactly what my mother used to say: "You have so many friends because *you are a friend.*"

Helping people gives me joy, and if it's appreciated, I'm always happy to give even more. As the Wizard of Oz said to the Tin Man, "Remember, my sentimental friend, one's heart is not judged by how much one loves, but by how much one is loved by others." That takes work, loyalty, and understanding. I'm convinced that we get from friendship what we put into friendship.

Mary, of course, is my best friend. There's no way that any of my life now would be possible without her. She is the heart and soul of our family, and the heart and soul of Sam Haskell. She is the dream come true. She is the mirror that I want to show a great image to, and she's also the safe haven that can help contain my warts and blemishes.

During my years as an executive at William Morris, I tried to attend every recital, every ball game, every school production that Sam IV and Mary Lane were in. But I couldn't be home for dinner as much as I would have liked. Still, Mary always made it work. When the kids were little, their bedtime was around eight or eight-thirty. She would always get them excited about my coming home to read stories. I'd climb into Sam's bed—he had a bunk bed with a double bed on bottom and a single on top—and the kids would jump in on either side of me. We called Sam's bed "The Cozy" because it was so cozy in there. Some nights all three of us fell asleep that way. Mary would have to come in and take Mary Lane to her bed, then me to mine.

The thing about Mary—and I will say this until I die—is that she never once made me feel bad about time not spent with her and the children. Because of her the kids understood that Daddy had a really hard job. But when we had vacation time or weekend time or reading time at night, that was their time and everyone knew nothing would get in the way.

Mary understood what being married to an agent meant, and many times the agents who worked for me would say, "You and Mary seem so happy together. My wife gripes at me all the time about having to work late or weekends or fly to Vegas or New York. How do you make it work?"

I'd tell them, "This works because Mary is so independent. She doesn't sit at home waiting for me to come and take her out. She's always had charity projects, acting jobs, commercial voice-overs, recording projects. She volunteers as the kids' music teacher at the elementary school and room mother at the secondary school. Sometimes it seems like she's got more to do every day than I do."

Marriages and friendships can get into trouble when one of the two parties gets bored or jealous and depends on the one who's not bored to make them happy. We have to be happy independently first. And we need something to look forward to each day. If we don't, we start finding fault with everything around us. One of Mary's many contributions to my happiness was to never make me feel guilty. She knew I felt guilty enough on my own, and didn't add to it. And I did the same for her when the situations were reversed.

Mary has always stood in the light, and I have been lucky to stand in her shadow. I've often joked and said that when I die, and I'm standing outside the Gates of Heaven, Mary will be sitting at the right hand of God—his good and faithful servant—and I'll tell Saint Peter, "I'm sure I'm on the list. Can you check it again? Okay, please tell Mary Haskell I'm out here. That's Mary right up there, standing in God's light. She knows me. I know she'll get me in."

My mother taught me that to have a friend you must be a friend. When I was six years old she took me, my best friend Randy Hollis, and four other boys to see Disney's *101 Dalmatians*. Randy got scared of Cruella de Vil, and my mother had to take him out, leaving the rest of us in the theater. Afterward I complained, "Why was Randy so scared? Why didn't he finish the movie?" I was frustrated he didn't stay for the end. "He was frightened of Cruella," she explained. "But he's your friend and you have to accept that. Don't be angry because he didn't finish the movie."

It's never been difficult for me to *be* a friend, and to honor this promise to my mother. But honestly, a whole chapter about what a good friend I've been is . . . well, not something even I would want to read. I'd rather celebrate the gifts of friendship I've been blessed with and demonstrate friendship in action, by example.

In January of 2005, one month after I'd left William Morris, my dear friend and former client, Emmy-winning producer George Schlatter, was contracted to produce the preinaugural gala honoring the second inauguration of President George W. Bush. George Schlatter and I had worked together on countless television projects for the past twenty-five years. Though he was like a father to me, I had never asked him for anything. Mary's first album for Concord Records was being released in March of that year. He knew we were looking for ways to promote the project, and out of the blue George called and said, "I have an idea that I'd like to run by you. Do you remember how Natalie Cole sang with the video of her father on 'Unforgettable'? I want to use the same process and have Mary sing 'America the Beautiful' with a video of Ray Charles for the President's preinaugural gala at the White House. What do you think?"

Mary and I were overjoyed at George's invitation. I had never wanted to be perceived as an agent who stood around holding a client's purse, but during the Gala, as host Ryan Seacrest was reading Mary's introduction, she leaned in to me and whispered, "Love, would you please hold my purse?" I was never so glad to hold a purse in my life. All I could think about, as Mary performed for President Bush and his family, was just how far we had come since our first date at the Pizza Hut in Oxford, Mississippi, so many years before.

I will always love George Schlatter for doing that for Mary. She literally brought the house down, and the President and the First Lady personally thanked her at the end of the evening.

———

When Hurricane Katrina struck the Gulf Coast in 2005, I'd been retired from William Morris for eight months. I wanted to do something to help the residents of Mississippi, who got less media attention than the victims in New Orleans—so I put together a show called "Mississippi Rising," and needed to get a lot of people and performers from California to Mississippi. Quickly.

Out of the blue, Steve Mosko, a business friend who runs Sony Television, offered me the Sony Jet. I might have asked for it eventually, but he beat me to it. He also threw in some cast members from *The Young and the Restless* and *Days of Our Lives,* which gave me eight more stars for my lineup.

When you're the guy who usually helps everyone and someone steps up out of the goodness of their heart to say, "Sam, can I do this for you?" all you can do is stand back and say, "Whoa!" And then, "Thanks!"

We all know what it feels like to love someone, but this is what it feels like to realize someone loves you.

Another friend, Steve Albright, also called while I was producing "Mississippi Rising," not to say, "Can I come?" but to announce "I'm coming with you and I want you to put me to work."

Steve understood the expression "to share time, talent, and treasure," but to me, sharing his time was the best example of philanthropy *and* friendship. I'll never forget that.

———

My mother believed in the *Reader's Digest* conviction that laughter is always the best medicine. She loved to laugh, and her friend Nadine Bryan, who recognized this trait in her, once did a needlepoint for my mother, "Let a smile be your umbrella." Laughter, my mother thought, would always wipe away the tears. "Try to find friends who can make you laugh," she would tell me and my brothers. "Laughter takes care of everything."

One of my best friends at Ole Miss was a beauty from Indianola named Marsha Hull. Marsha and her boyfriend, Frank Tindall (now her husband), were Mary and my best friends in college, and they are our best friends today.

Along with Mary and me, Marsha was a member of "The Group," the University of Mississippi's song-and-dance team and recruitment ambassadors.

We traveled all over the state to our "group" concerts using our own cars. Marsha's was the most popular, and I always rode shotgun with her. The only drawback was that Marsha was always late. She ran thirty minutes behind everyone else. Frank called it "Marsha Time."

To catch up, she'd always drive fast. Even if our destination was an hour and a half away, she could leave an hour before the concert and still make it. Marsha's secret? She had a Fuzzbuster that would beep if a highway patrolman was anywhere nearby. She could go as fast as she wanted on those back roads, and we'd always make it, laughing all the way.

One night, we were really, really late, and Marsha drove really, really fast. Suddenly we saw the lights of a highway patrol car behind us. Marsha's Fuzzbuster hadn't gone off. We pulled over, and as Marsha rolled down the window, she held the Fuzzbuster, swinging, by the cord. Before the highway patrolman took out his ticket book, she said, "Before you write that ticket, how much will you give me for a broken Fuzzbuster?" He laughed so hard he couldn't—and didn't—give her a ticket. When she told him where we were going, he told us he was a big Ole Miss fan—and gave us a police escort to the concert.

———

There's nothing like a friend who believes in you and is willing to show it when others won't.

When I decided to head for Los Angeles after college, I'd spent all my summer savings on a car. I needed a loan to cover the trip and a couple of months' rent and food. I went to someone I had trusted and respected all of my life, and asked to borrow the money. He turned me down, saying that I had no business moving to California. "You should just get a job," he said. I was shocked, but not discouraged. He was a friend of my father's, and he sounded just like him. My mother and Aunt Betty couldn't believe it.

Fortunately, I knew someone else I hoped *did* believe in me: my high school football coach, Earl Stevens. After I explained my situation, he gave me a thousand dollars and wished me well. I promised to pay him back in a year, with interest.

I managed to return all the money to Coach Stevens and his wife, Lazette, within a year—with extra interest. And I sent them a nice Tiffany bowl as soon as I could—an additional thanks for believing in me.

———

In show business—or any business—we're typically cautioned not to think of our bosses, clients, competition, or coworkers as friends; we're told it's a *business* relationship without personal depth. We're warned that it will change when one party moves on, gets a promotion, or leaves the company. You might stay in touch and be cordial, you may even work together again; but otherwise the intimate aspects are over. You don't vacation together. Dinners stop. If your kids are in the same school you might wave to each other at back-to-school night.

You just can't take it personally.

Maybe this is often true, but not always. You *can* create genuine friendships in business. My mother had some rules of friendship that I follow to this day: Never start a relationship thinking about what you can get—start by asking yourself what the other person needs. Make that person laugh. Give advice and counsel if needed. Help in any way you can. You never know what will happen, and what you get back is the icing on the cake.

My mother treated both her friends and her acquaintances this way, and she was beloved for it.

As for me, even if the friendship doesn't extend beyond the office, the relationship can be genuine in its context. And given enough time, you can really expand your love and knowledge of that person. In fact, I believe that if friendship and business can be intertwined, the emergent partnership is stronger.

I've been friends with Les Moonves, CBS president and CEO, for almost thirty years, and we've been through a lot together. I met Les in 1980, when he was head of development for a tiny production company working on the Columbia Pictures lot. I had just become a full-fledged agent, and I took him to breakfast to see if we could find projects to work on together. I felt an instant connection. We got each other. But as we were both low-level executives just finding our way, we spent most of our time talking not about business, but about our lives—where we were from, our aspirations, and how we could make sure we'd be successful doing things together. Our friendship grew as the years passed.

When, in 1990, NBC's Warren Littlefield wanted to develop a series about a family he knew growing up who had four daughters with boy's names—Teddy, Alex, Georgie, and Frankie—my clients Ron Cowen and Daniel Lipman were tasked with creating it. They had just won an Emmy for writing the movie *An Early Frost*. The series, *Sisters*, debuted in 1991 starring Swoosie Kurtz, Sela Ward, Julianne Phillips, and Patricia Kalember. Mary did a couple of seasons as a recurring character. Ashley Judd was discovered on the show, as well as Paul Rudd and Eric Close, who is now on *Without a Trace*.

Lorimar TV, which was run by Les Moonves, produced.

When Sela Ward's character, Teddy, needed a boyfriend, Les Moonves called me with an idea to cast this good-looking young man, a William Morris client, who'd made many, many pilots and had been on several series that never quite took off. His last steady work had been on *Facts of Life* and a few episodes of *Roseanne,* but Moonves had kept him under contract at the studio for several years believing he would one day become a big star. His name was George Clooney. Moonves asked me to send his audition tape to Cowen and Lipman and the third executive producer TV legend Michael Filerman. Michael, Ron and Dan loved Clooney's quality and immediately cast him as Sela Ward's love interest, Detective James Falconer. He did nineteen episodes.

When problems arose, my friendships—especially with Les Moonves—helped solve them. For instance, when we sold the pilot for *Sisters,* Swoosie Kurtz, who'd just won an Emmy, was the show's top-billed actress. But we almost didn't get the deal made because Swoosie wouldn't sign her contract unless she had a private bathroom attached to her dressing room. Stall or no stall, she didn't want to sit down next to somebody else.

I kept saying, "She's got to have a private bathroom," and Les Moonves kept saying, "No." Everyone else's deals were done, and he wanted hers finished too. Every day I'd visit Swoosie's primary agent at William Morris and beg her to close the deal, but she couldn't: Swoosie wanted what she wanted and she was willing to lose the show over it. NBC called every day. Cowen and Lipman were getting nervous as the start of production crept closer and closer.

Les called me, frustrated out of his mind. "This is ridiculous!" he said. "No one on this lot has a private bathroom! Swoosie's deal *must* close!"

Because I knew Moonves well, I could make an unusual suggestion.

"What if I can find a performer who does?"

"Does what?"

"Have a private bathroom on the lot."

"If you can find someone who has a private bathroom on our lot," he said, taking up the challenge, "then I'll give Swoosie a bathroom."

I did some digging and discovered that Patti LuPone, whose *Life Goes On* was a Warner Bros. show shot *on the same lot* (Lorimar and Warner Bros. were sister companies that would soon merge), had her own bathroom.

So I went back to Moonves. "Patti LuPone has one."

Maybe he wondered whether I'd be able to meet his challenge in the first place, but to his credit, Les kept his word and gave Swoosie her bathroom. All the other "Sisters" got one too. I guess it was all about the cost of construction. Afterward, as thanks, Swoosie Kurtz sent me a miniature ceramic toilet with flowers in it.

In 1995, after Moonves left Warner Bros. to become president of CBS, he needed a favor. By then, Moonves had become my most important friend in the business. We had both come a long way from our first meeting at Art's Deli in Studio City. We had great lunches and dinners every other month. He came to my Christmas parties. It was still a work relationship, but it didn't hurt that we also liked the Hell out of each other. In fact, when someone needed something from Moonves, they often came to me for help. They knew he trusted me. He knew I kept my word. And if he needed something at William Morris, he knew I would do everything I could to give it to him.

"Sam," he said, "this is the Tiffany network, I need to rebuild it, and to do that I need a show with America's most beloved guy. What do I have to do to get Bill Cosby?"

William Morris chairman Norman Brokaw was Cosby's main agent at William Morris. Because Norman trusted me, he let me create a relationship with his most important client and allowed me to make the deals. Cosby wanted to do another sitcom. Frankly, NBC was the natural choice, since he'd been there with *The Cosby Show* and *The Cosby Mysteries*. The producers, Marcy Carsey and Tom Werner, leaned toward ABC, since they had great relationships there because of their megahit *Roseanne*. Based on my friendship with Moonves, I wanted to give CBS a shot. But I also believed CBS was the right place. I knew Moonves would try harder and give the show every chance to succeed whether the ratings were initially there or not—an uncommon occurrence in the highly competitive network ratings race.

Norman Brokaw put me on the phone with Cosby to go over the offers we had received from every network. Because of my accent, and my being Norman's lieutenant, Bill called me "Deputy Dawg." I said, "If all things are equal financially, I believe we should be at CBS, because you will be the most important person in Les Moonves's stable. There's something to be said for that." I also told him that I thought Moonves had great character. Bill trusted me. We made an unprecedented two-year deal, for starters, and the new *Cosby* series stayed on the air for four seasons. Most important, though, Brokaw and I made sure that Cosby and Moonves developed a strong relationship based on loyalty and trust.

Les also ordered a new pilot based on the Art Linkletter series *Kids Say the Darndest Things.* The host was none other than Bill Cosby. The series lasted five seasons on CBS, and seven-year-old Mary Lane Haskell was one of the four kids chosen to be interviewed in the premiere episode.

That same year, we sold CBS on a young comedian named Ray Romano, and the pilot for *Everybody Loves Raymond,* written by Phil Rosenthal. CBS ordered the series and scheduled it on Friday night the first season. It got great reviews, but very few people were watching. Bill Cosby called me and said, "I want to talk to Les Moonves about Ray Romano. See if you can get him on the phone, right now."

I could always get Les on the phone, so we called and Cosby said, "I love this man Ray Romano. You put him behind me on Monday night, and that show will work. We're compatible."

Moonves thought it was a great idea, and history confirms it, because on the heels of *Cosby, Raymond* just took off. When I look back on my entertainment career, I can honestly say that *Everybody Loves Raymond* is the project that I am most proud of. Several of the cast members—Ray, Doris Roberts, Brad Garrett, and Patricia Heaton—became four of my dearest friends. *Raymond* was a perfect part of my life.

The older we get, the harder it is to make friends. Trust and a connection are hard to come by when we're preoccupied with life, and as a result we are less open.

The relationship with my client Ray Romano took a long time to develop. Like many talented and successful actors, he had a protective exterior because he had been taught to believe that agents are only your friend when they think they're going to make a commission.

When the pilot for *Everybody Loves Raymond* was put together, I had never met him. (Ray lived on the East Coast.) But because I was the packager and I was the closest person to Les Moonves at CBS, Ray's agent in our New York office asked me to keep a protective eye on the project.

During those early years, Ray and his wife, Anna, looked at me as "The Suit." They were always polite, but I don't think they ever understood why I showed up everywhere. When the TV Academy honored the cast and producers of *Raymond,* I was there. When Ray did charity work, I was there. I didn't have to go. It wasn't about making money. I just wanted him to know I was supportive. When Ray got his very first Emmy nomination, I sent a big gift basket to their house. On Emmy night, Anna said, "Thanks for the basket—I'm sure you didn't even know you sent it." That stung. But I understood. She thought my assistant had done it, just as a matter of course, and that the intent was "just something I needed to do." I said, "No, no, I chose everything in there; I do that for all the people I care about. Did you like the Cabernet? Did you like the Gruyère?"

That turned a corner with Anna, but Ray was still a bit remote. I guessed that he just couldn't trust that I wasn't simply a flesh-peddling predator who cared only about the money. But because I showed up for the tapings of at least two shows a month, I think he finally began to believe I might have had other motivations. I'd hang out on the set with Ray's manager, Rory Rosegarten, and Les Moonves's brother, attorney Jon Moonves, both close friends of mine. I'd say hello to Ray and never pushed to try and have a personal conversation. Then one night, the show stopped for an hour while they did a hurried rewrite, and Ray invited me to his dressing room. We started talking about our kids. We scheduled a lunch at the Warner Bros. commissary. Then Mary and I were invited to a function at his house. Soon after, Ray and Anna came to our house, and it was just the four of us. But again, the relationship evolved only to a point.

A longtime friend of mine, the comedian/director Wil Shriner, was hired to direct three episodes of *Raymond* during the sixth season. I took him aside and said, "Wil, I need to get to the next level with Ray. I know that he likes you a lot. Do you think that you and your girlfriend could invite me and Mary and Ray and Anna to a dinner? I think if *you* set it up, not us, that would say something to him."

Wil did it, and the dinner was a success. After that, Ray and I talked more often. When he agreed to come to Mississippi in 2002 to host "Stars Over Mississippi," it was finally a lock. We got each other, and he trusted me. We had the same values, and Anna and Mary were practically the same person.

I wanted to be Ray's friend because I liked him. I thought he was cool, funny, and a truly great guy. My mother used to say, "Surround yourself with people who make you better." Maybe Ray's resisting made me want to be his friend more too. Maybe it was the challenge. I just know I was drawn to him, but it took a great effort on my part to become his friend.

————

Sometimes friends can make a dream come true.

Every once in a while in business, especially show business, you've been a lifelong fan of a client you also someday represent. It wouldn't matter if he or she were your client, you'd still love them because they'd made a personal and emotional impact on you, sometimes long before you got into the business. That you get to work together just enhances the possibility that you can have more than a business relationship.

While I became great friends with clients like Kathie Lee

Gifford and Debbie Allen after moving to L.A., I discovered Dolly Parton when I was only ten years old. She sang on Porter Wagoner's TV show. She was so pretty and talented. Even my parents liked the show.

On Dolly's final episode of the show, she sang "I Will Always Love You." People think it's Whitney Houston's song, from her movie *The Bodyguard,* but Dolly wrote it for Porter Wagoner as a good-bye and a thank-you for his help in getting her established.

When I was a college senior in 1977, Dolly had her first big national interview, with Barbara Walters, who asked, "What do you really aspire to?"

"I want to do movies, television, Broadway," Dolly said. "I want to be a superstar!"

A bold statement for a country singer with big hair and all the rest to make on national television. What guts! Even though she had a very secure job in Nashville, her own hit show the year before, and was all over the music awards, she had an even bigger dream to follow. Maybe I loved Dolly because I had big dreams too.

In 1982 I helped package the *Golden Globe Awards* on CBS. I was so excited, not only because I would get to meet all the movie stars who attended, but because "Nine to Five" had been nominated as the best song of the year, and Dolly Parton had agreed to perform it on the show.

The awards were staged at the Beverly Hilton Hotel. Once again, Bob Precht was the producer. He invited me in for a meeting with Robert Preston, from *The Music Man,* who was hosting with Kate Jackson, from *Charlie's Angels.* I was in Preston's dressing room when I heard that Dolly Parton had arrived. I ran into the showroom and found her sitting at a table in front of the stage, wearing a red-sequined dress. Rehearsals were running behind, so I sat down and introduced myself.

"I'm Sam Haskell, from William Morris. I'm the packaging

agent for the Golden Globes. We represent the Hollywood For-
eign Press Association, and I helped sell the show to CBS. I've
seen *Nine to Five* and I've watched you since I was a kid growing
up in Mississippi."

"Mississippi?" she said. That impressed her more than anything else I'd mentioned. She was accustomed to all these slick
New York and Los Angeles agents and managers.

"Yes ma'am."

"Yes ma'am!" she echoed, and started laughing. "I feel like I'm
back in Tennessee. We're too close in age for you to say 'Yes
ma'am' to me!"

"Whatever you say, Ms. Parton," I said.

"No, no. You call me Dolly. All my friends call me Dolly."

"Yes, Dolly."

"So you work at William Morris."

"Yes, Dolly."

"Did you start in the mailroom?"

"I did."

We had a lovely talk that lasted until she had to rehearse her
song, and that was the last time we spoke for almost ten years.

By 1992, I'd earned enough credibility in the business to be
able to pursue the big talents, and I kept after Dolly's managers to
let me represent her. Eventually, when Dolly wanted to change
agencies, we got a chance to meet again. At the meeting I told her
I had continued to follow her every move and had seen all of her
movies. I tried to sell her on the idea of building her existing production company into an even bigger success, to come up with
projects for her to star in, and to enable her to executive-produce.
Unfortunately, I didn't seal the deal. Dolly went elsewhere.

Six years later I got a call from her manager, Jim Morey, by
then a longtime personal friend whose daughters had babysat my
kids. "We're taking meetings for Dolly Parton again, and I want
you to be the first."

"Thank you."

"I believe from the way she felt about you last time that we might only have to meet with *you*. That's the goal."

This time, when I walked in, Dolly stood up and hugged me. "I remember you! Sit down and let's visit. We have a lot to talk about."

True to Jim Morey's hope, the meeting went wonderfully and she canceled the rest of her meetings. Dolly Parton had finally become my client.

I threw myself into my work for her, and we spent countless hours together in a way that reinforced my belief that I could mix business with friendship. Mary and I flew with the children to Dollywood and got our own private tour. We stayed at Dolly's ranch in the Tennessee mountains where she grew up. She performed at one of my "Stars Over Mississippi" benefit concerts. She also wanted to meet my extended family and friends when she was in Amory. At times I felt as if I were bringing a girlfriend home from college—only it was Dolly Parton!

Dolly also loved my children. She took Mary Lane to her Malibu beach house and they played "dress-up." Mary Lane would come back to us with makeup and long fingernails. She took Sam shopping and bought him games. She even let Mary record a song she'd written, called "Try," which Dolly hadn't let any other artist use because she was saving it for herself. "Try" became the first track on Mary's album, *Inspired*.

As our friendship grew, Dolly and I confided everything in each other. I would go to her house on the way home from work, and when I was on the low-carb Atkins Diet she'd fix me a whole dinner of protein. Or if I'd had a rough day, she'd fix me fried chicken and mashed potatoes because that was the comfort food my mother used to make for me.

Hanging out in Dolly's kitchen, I learned a lot about relationships and life. We also talked politics and about celebrities who were in the rag sheets—even stories about her. Dolly gave me advice on raising the children, being a good husband, what clients expected from their agents, and how to be a good person.

We talked about the challenges that our families have caused us. Hers had to do with growing up in Sevierville, Tennessee, in the Smoky Mountains, living in poverty, kids four or five to a bed. She took care of the little ones, because her mother just didn't have time. And then, when Dolly graduated from high school, she went straight to Nashville—and several of her younger siblings moved with her. She raised them as if they were her children: sent them to school and paid their way. To this day, those siblings think of her as their mother. Their children, instead of calling her Aunt Dolly, call her Aunt Granny.

We had many, many conversations about the obstacles put before her and everything she did to get around them. This led to talk about the promises I made to my mother. "I'll bet you had a Donna Reed mother, a Ward Cleaver father, and a white picket fence. You must have had the perfect life," she said.

"Oh no I didn't," I replied. Then I told her my story—all about my father, my parents' divorce, my struggles to get to California, withdrawing from law school, and my early financial woes. It was her turn to be surprised. Afterward, we seemed closer. We had both experienced adversity in our lives, and it was good to know that we had both struggled through and succeeded by controlling our own destinies.

When we are lucky enough, through our life's journey, to befriend people who *also* befriend and mentor our children, well, that's just about the most awesome thing I can think of. Every special person mentioned in this book has loved Sam IV and Mary Lane from the very moment they entered this world. But Emmy-winning actress Doris Roberts has connected with my children as a loving grandmother might have connected with them. She has taught them both about hope. She has shared ideas of building confidence and self-esteem with them. She took Mary Lane under her wing as an actress after she saw Mary Lane's performance as Dolly Levi in her high school production of *Hello, Dolly!* Doris recognized some of herself in Mary Lane, and has been a wise and trusted adviser to her. Mary Lane and Sam both love "Aunt Doris," and Mary and I cherish the impact that she has had on all of our lives!

———

A friend can sometimes take the place of missing parents. To have that deep an understanding with a friend is a blessing.

I met Erik Sterling and Jason Winters in 1988, when my client Morgan Fairchild was interested in signing with their management and production team, the Sterling Winters Company. Jason, an African-American Christian, and I were the same age. Erik was debonair, white, and Jewish. They were also a couple.

Little did I know that they would soon become two of the most important relationships I'd ever have, both professionally and personally. We ended up sharing several other clients together—Joan van Ark, Swoosie Kurtz, Marilyn McCoo, Billy Davis, Jr., and Kathy Ireland—but the most rewarding benefit of our relationship was a profound friendship that also included their business partners—and adopted sons—Jon Carrasco and Stephen Roseberry. We love people for lots of reasons, but the most important one is because you realize, without a shadow of a doubt, that you are loved in return. I know that if anything bad were to ever happen to me or my family, many people would rush to the house to see about us, but Jason and Erik would already be there to open the door and welcome them in. For the past twenty years, there has not been a special moment that we haven't shared with Erik, Jason, Jon, and Stephen. That includes their producing two successful Christmas movies, *Once Upon a Christmas* and *Twice Upon a Christmas,* starring Kathy Ireland, John Dye, and Mary Donnelly Haskell. (Since then, Kathy has become one of our dearest friends.) *Twice Upon a Christmas* was even screened at a special event for First Lady Laura Bush at the White House.

Erik and Jason were also my most intimate council during the last five difficult years before I left William Morris. I would call Jason at least once a week and ask him to meet me at our favorite restaurant in Beverly Hills, RJ's the Rib Joint, where we would pig out on barbecued ribs, corn on the cob, baked potatoes, and chocolate cake and ice cream. I needed comfort food and a welcome ear, and Jason provided both, never once letting me pick up the bill. He understood the nature of each player in the chess game that was William Morris, and he helped me process the moves I'd have to make. I have never doubted Erik's or Jason's character. Their only agenda, then and now, is to make life better for their clients and friends.

It's almost as if they picked up where my mother left off.

I needed that, especially then, and, as best friends do, they understood that without my having to ask.

SIX

Always Seek Understanding

Without understanding, problems are difficult to solve.

—MARY KIRKPATRICK HASKELL

When I was in the fourth grade, my teacher, Mrs. Jane Camp, gave me a B in English. I had always made straight As, and I was so disappointed that I complained to my mother, "Why did Mrs. Camp give me a B, when all I've ever made is an A?"

"Did you work hard and do everything Mrs. Camp asked you to do?" she asked.

"Yes." And I had. Not knowing why I'd gotten only a B was confusing and frustrating.

Rather than do what many parents do today—rush in and question or berate the teacher because little Johnny's self-esteem is too important to crush—my mother told me that she didn't know whether or not the grade was fair, and that *I* needed to talk to Mrs. Camp about what she had done. "Go ask her why," she said.

"Me?"

"Yes. You need to understand why."

The next day after school I talked to Mrs. Camp. Afterward she reevaluated my work and changed my grade to an A. Honestly, I don't know if she found an error in her grade book, or if I had been persuasive, or what, but she did thank me for the polite way I'd handled the situation before sending me on my way. Even if Mrs. Camp hadn't changed my grade, my disappointment would have been tempered because I'd left her classroom knowing that by going to see her personally, I'd made it possible for her to listen to my side and, I hoped, to understand. And I had gotten the chance to hear her thoughts on my grammar and class participation as well.

My mother believed in confronting situations you don't understand, seeing circumstances from other people's points of view, and asking people what they mean and why they've done what they've done. She explained that even though we might not like what we learn, we'll at least get the information necessary to help us move on. Doing nothing is the wrong answer, whatever the outcome.

You can just refuse to compromise, misinterpret, miscommunicate, and doubt yourself. You can get so angry you say or do something you regret, or hold it in and let it fester. Neither response is healthy. Who needs an ulcer?

When we're at a fork in the road, we need the wisdom to be able to understand where both roads lead in order to make authentic forward progress. Yogi Berra put it this way: "When you come to a fork in the road, take it." In other words, life moves ahead and you have to move with it. That's why my mother prompted me to step up and find out what Mrs. Camp had to say, and as I grew older I realized the goal was not to simply get my way but to grab ahold of the truths revealed by friction, and find either a compromise or acceptance.

It's all about understanding. And sometimes the will to understand leads to the solution itself.

From that day in fourth grade on, I promised my mother that when facing conflicts I'd always seek understanding first and then act. Now I often say, "Help me understand this because I can't help you [or us] unless I do." I may not get an immediate answer, but if I'm persistent and courteous, most people will finally come around. Being direct and plainspoken usually gets a positive response because it short-circuits game playing. When self-interest and the interests of others come together, honest and effective communication leads to results.

Like all lessons, this one came often and in many forms, some indelible.

My mother grew up in modest circumstances in Amory and had always dreamed of owning a certain house in town. Thanks to my father's business success, he bought that home when my brothers and I were young. It was close to fifty years old, and came with almost an acre of land.

Gigantic old oak trees dotted our yard, and every fall the grounds were completely covered with leaves. My father would divide the yard into three sections, one each for me and my brothers, and every Saturday we had to rake our sections, then pack up the leaves and get them out to the street so the city could haul them away.

The job could take all day—if you let it. I would rather have been at the local movie theater, where, for fifty cents, I could see a double feature. So each Saturday I would set the alarm for six o'clock in the morning so that I could have my raking done by ten and make it to the movies in time. My brothers would sleep in until noon and goof off, so that it took them the rest of the day. We all had to be finished by dinnertime, when my dad got back from the golf course, or we'd be punished.

One day, after I did my raking and went to the movies as usual, my brothers decided to rake all their leaves into my section. I got home at six o'clock, just as my father pulled up. Jamie and Billy stood outside, waiting, acting proud that they had finished their work.

When my father saw that my section was still covered with leaves, my brothers said, "Sammy's been at the movies all day."

Without stopping to consider that I'd always done my work early and that I wasn't the type to be so irresponsible and disrespectful, my father was ready to whip me with his belt.

"But you don't understand!" I protested. "I finished mine this morning. They must have raked all their leaves into my section!"

My mother and my aunt Betty were in our kitchen having coffee, and they assured my father that I was telling the truth. My father said it didn't matter and used his belt on all three of us: my brothers for raking their leaves into my section, and me for tattling.

That made no sense. If I hadn't told the truth, then he wouldn't have known I'd raked my section.

I couldn't get over my father's having punished me for nothing. Plus he wanted me to rake the leaves—Billy and Jamie's leaves—off my section *again*. While my aunt Betty fumed, my mother—who had cried over my father's irrational behavior—told me, "Go back out there and rerake your section of the yard."

"But why?" I said. I was determined to refuse. It just wasn't fair. But my mother knew that she had to make me understand why I had to listen to my father even though she didn't personally support him.

"The only way you can make it right for your father is to show him that you raked. The only way to make it right for your brothers is to set a positive example. Remember what I told you about trying to understand how everyone else feels? You don't have to give up what you believe, but by understanding what they need, and what in the long run will be good for you, you're going to learn something. I promise."

I'd been honest. I'd done my best. I learned that sometimes understanding meant turning the other cheek. I had to see it from my father's point of view, no matter how little it made sense, then let go of the unfairness and not hold on to that horrible moment. I went back outside to rake those leaves again . . . and within five minutes my brothers, who had started to feel bad about what they had done, came out to help me. Momma had been right!

———

My mother told me more than once that being judgmental could prevent me from understanding a situation in its entirety. But again, that was a lesson I'd have to learn on my own—and in a very public way.

When I was a senior in high school, I was at football practice one afternoon. We had lost a big game the Friday night before, and everyone on the team groused about whose fault it was. I was certain that the Amory Panthers' linemen (me among them) had done their job but that the backs had fumbled, dropped punt returns, and missed passes. The backs blamed us. And everyone blamed the defense.

The coach decided to reverse our positions in order to make us understand and appreciate what our fellow players went through. Linemen would learn how difficult it was to run the ball, and backs would learn how difficult it was to block. I was sent downfield for the kickoff, and the ball came right for me. I looked up, praying, "God, please don't let me drop this football . . . please." At that exact moment I saw a lone bird flying overhead. Then I heard a "plop" and realized he'd relieved himself right onto my helmet's face mask. I fell to the ground moaning, and the goo dripped into my mouth. I threw up. The coach ran over to see what was wrong, and I screamed, "A bird has just s**t into my face." The team fell to the grass, laughing. So did the coaching staff, who realized the lesson was over, sent us to the showers, and called it a day.

As for me, I now understood that everyone had a tough job and that I should focus on my own performance instead of complaining about someone else's. Since then I've been reluctant to criticize, especially when I'm not inside a building.

————

Like all relationships, marriage requires great heaps of understanding in the most basic ways.

When Mary and I were first married she would leave her shoes by whatever door she used to walk into the house. Mary has lots of shoes, so there would be five or six pairs scattered around. I'm a neat freak. After six months I said, "Love [as we've always called each other], why don't you just put these little piles of shoes in the closet?" Without missing a beat she said, "If these little piles of shoes weren't here, you'd miss them." Meaning, if she weren't here, I'd miss her. You know what? I found I could live with a few shoes here and there.

Later, when we had little Sam, suddenly "kid junk" was everywhere: bottles and swings, strollers and diapers, toys and playpens. This new mess tested me more than Mary's shoes had. I wanted everything put away. Naturally, it couldn't be. To survive, I had to reach a compromise *with myself* between my desire for neatness and the impossibility of finding order in the situation. When Mary Lane came along the next year, if I couldn't find a spot to sit on the sofa, I'd just push all the crap aside and sit down. When the kids got older, we reintroduced order and began to make them put their things away. Mary even began closeting her shoes, because with the kids' stuff everywhere there was such a thing as too much of a mess. And I realized that someone else's needs are sometimes more important than my own. You just can't "sweat the small stuff."

———

Oftentimes, I have worked so closely with a client that it's almost like a marriage, in all but a few obvious ways. Plus, each client comes with a mix-and-match assortment of the following: spouse, adviser, manager, hairdresser, physical trainer, driver, cook, psychic, relatives . . . you get the picture. When a compromise must be sought, it's often these satellite folks who require it most.

Usually it's the spouse.

I met Kathie Lee Gifford (then Johnson) in 1978 when I came to Los Angeles. She was the *Name That Tune* girl. She was engaging, pretty, talented, and funny. Brassy and ballsy, too. She just had something. I thought she could be a big star, but I was still in the mailroom. I said, "When I become an agent, you're going to be my first client." We had been introduced by Susie Cole, whose brother, Byars, was one of my Sigma Chi fraternity brothers at Ole Miss. Susie was Kathie's assistant, and we occasionally "house-sat" her home in Woodland Hills while Kathie was performing in Reno, Nevada, at Harrah's. From the moment I met Kathie I felt a connection. She was always full of questions about the business, and I tried to answer every one of them.

I was promoted May 10, 1980, and, the day after she signed with me.

Kathie wanted to be an actress, but we weren't having much success. She auditioned to be Farrah Fawcett's replacement in the ABC series *Charlie's Angels,* but she didn't get the part. The casting director actually told Kathie that she was not pretty enough, and Kathie's response was "Let me know when you're casting a cartoon." When I heard about a guest-host opening for a week on *A.M. L.A.,* I convinced her to try out. She nailed the audition and got the job. When the people at ABC in New York saw her, they thought she might also make a great substitute for Joan Lunden on *Good Morning America* when Joan went on maternity leave. Soon she was a *Good Morning America* correspondent. When Joan Lunden got pregnant again, Kathie replaced her for two months. Then Regis saw her—and the rest is TV history.

After Kathie Lee Johnson met Frank Gifford on *Good Morning America,* she told me, "You've got to watch the show this morning. Frank Gifford cohosted and he was so charming."

They became friends, he took her to lunch with Don Meredith, and he took her to dinner. Four years later, suddenly they're dating. Then before you could say, "what happened?" they were married, and I could no longer call her as much as I once did. It came as no surprise that soon Frank wanted to have lunch alone—to lay down the rules about how things were going to be with me and Kathie Lee now that he was in the picture.

"I know you and Kathie are friends," he said, "but I don't want you calling the house after five o'clock New York time."

"But that's two in the afternoon Los Angeles time," I said. "My day is only half over."

Didn't matter. Frank was suspicious of agents. To him they were money-hungry flesh peddlers. He also had other frustrating restrictions and was testy with me a couple of times. But I never fought back or confronted him; instead I tried to see it from his point of view, because I knew I'd need to prove to him I wouldn't be a threat.

While I had admired Frank Gifford as an athlete for years, it seemed he had a problem not only with me, but with anyone who was a significant part of Kathie's life before he appeared on the scene. When I flew into New York once a month to visit her at the show and go to lunch and talk about all the offers I had for her, I'm sure he got tired of later hearing, "Sam thinks this" or "Sam thinks that." Kathie was in a tough position. She could easily handle herself, but Frank was very protective.

She asked me to be patient, respect his position. I didn't like it, but I understood. I also took some comfort in Kathie's reassurances that she'd *never* let me be cut out of her life.

But one day Kathie called to tell me how frustrated she was with many of the other agents at the William Morris Agency, and felt it was time to make a change. I knew it was Frank's influence at the time, but it was devastating to me nonetheless. Apparently it was for Kathie, too, because six months later she was back.

She knew I'd do anything for her, and that I was there to help her get what she wanted and achieve her dreams. Going forward, we made six Christmas specials in a row. I wanted to get her into a sitcom, but we could never work it out given her schedule, and by the time she left the show with Regis, she'd started writing and composing Broadway musicals.

To be honest, I think Frank wanted Kathie to leave Regis because it took her away from him and the children, but she said it was totally her decision. She called me many times to express the heartbreak of being falsely accused of labor abuses, only to be devastated by Frank's infidelity a year later. Then when her beloved father, Eppie, was diagnosed with a terminal disease, Lewy body dementia, she couldn't go through another public, painful ordeal. She never announced the real reason, but I knew, and although I thought she might one day regret it, I understood, too. Kathie and I have always shared the same belief, that your career is the way you make your living but your family and faith are your life. Kathie loves Frank and she forgave him, but she was able to take the upper hand where her career was concerned, and suddenly I could call anytime I wanted to. To his credit, Frank has evolved. He's different now. And he's treated me well.

Now, of course, Kathie is back on the air, cohosting the last hour of *The Today Show* on NBC. We have been dear friends and business partners for over thirty years, even through a few bumps in the road. I like to think it's because we have always sought to understand both life's situations and each other. For Kathie and me, respect, love, and understanding have always gone hand in hand. I will always adore her!

———

The willingness to seek understanding allows relationships, careers, and life in general to work better than they would if we stayed attached to one strict way of behaving without considering the alternatives. If you can't understand, adapt, and change, you're doomed to repeat the same behaviors and get the same nonresults. Einstein said that's the definition of insanity, right?

Occasionally I've had to go to unusual lengths to find understanding.

When John Agoglia was the head of business affairs at NBC, I was William Morris's liaison to the network. Every deal I made for a client or a series ended up on Agoglia's desk.

He treated me horribly. He didn't return phone calls in a timely manner, he was not collaborative, he never allowed me to win anything, and I just felt that he flat out didn't like me worth a damn.

One day, while I was walking around the Paramount lot with a couple of friends, we passed some big display cases that contained Oscars won by the studio, and some old movie costumes. I pointed at one, a Revolutionary War uniform, that was all shot up and covered with bloody bullet holes and burns.

"Oh my God!" I thought—out loud. "That's the suit I wore last week during my meeting with John Agoglia!"

I had no idea why Agoglia was so contentious with me. What had I done? Why didn't he like me? I needed desperately to understand and resolve the situation, so I bought him a gift and asked to have a meeting. When he opened the box, he saw two pairs of boxing gloves. "Let's put them on," I said. "We obviously have a problem, and it's time to figure out what it is and settle it."

Agoglia didn't take it as a serious invitation to box, but he got the message. He said, "You know what? Everybody else likes you and gives you what you want. I figured I needed to be the other side of that." We did try on the gloves, though, then put them aside and shared a good laugh.

Now we were getting somewhere. He wanted to help me understand.

"I just want to make a good deal," I explained. "I'm not here to take advantage of you. I want to make a deal where I'm happy and you're happy. And I want to be your friend."

From then on, though he didn't just roll over and give me whatever I wanted, the anger and questioning were gone. I had been direct, we understood each other, and we have remained friends ever since.

———

When I was at William Morris, I wanted to share my mother's lesson about understanding with as many people as possible. We used to have retreat sessions for the television department on the last weekend in June, after pilot and staffing season was over and we'd booked our writers, producers, and actors into their TV jobs for the fall. Over time these retreats became very successful. After a couple of years we were inviting every department: legal, accounting, motion pictures, commercials, music. Then the William Morris board members wanted to come.

For years the retreats took place at a resort hotel in Ojai, California. (We tried Las Vegas once, but the city was too distracting!) Aside from the main sessions, we'd have a guest lecturer on Friday night—sometimes they were my mentors like Brandon

Tartikoff or the legendary network president Fred Silverman, or someone like current Disney Company chairman Bob Iger, or motivational giant Tony Robbins. On Saturday afternoon and evening we held the William Morris Olympics. We'd stage games, scavenger hunts, and athletic events. Everyone participated.

At the retreats, which I led, I committed myself to sharing the principle of seeking understanding with my coworkers because I believed it would create a better work environment, not only within the building but when our agents interacted with the rest of the entertainment community as well. We needed it because the normal way of doing business in Hollywood was to be secretive and competitive and to look for the best deal no matter what. I wanted to make good deals, but knowing that not everyone could get their way all the time, I wanted to create an atmosphere that maximized acceptance and collegiality.

First, I encouraged attendees to think about their IQ and EQ: intelligence quotient and emotional quotient. I asked them to talk about their strengths and their weaknesses. I'd divide the room into six discussion groups, and after ten minutes ask members of each group to talk about whether they felt dispensable or indispensable. I once asked everyone to discuss this line: "Youth is not a time of life, it is a state of mind. It is not a matter of rosy cheeks, red lips, and supple knees, it's a matter of the will." I posed the question: "What great thing would you attempt to accomplish if you knew you would not fail?"

I kept noticing that coworkers were sometimes furious at one another's success and happy about their failures. This concerned me more than anything. So I reminded them, "It's the character of very few men to honor without envy a friend who has prospered." Then I would ask each person to tell me about someone they were close to who was more successful than they were, and someone who was less successful—and why they were friends with each. Most chose people outside the room: a family member, a classmate. We aired out the topics of jealousy and competition.

I would ask participants to share a story about themselves that they'd never told anyone. One guy, from our literary department in New York, was gay. He said that one Saturday when he was thirteen years old, his father walked in from playing golf and saw him huddled in the den, watching Gene Tierney in *Laura*. The boy thought the movie was the most glorious thing he'd ever seen. His father was furious. He turned off the TV set and threw him out into the yard and said, "Go play ball!" The man confided, "I think my father knew then that I was gay, but he couldn't face it."

Once a participant had shared something private, the other people in the room started raising their hands and telling their most intimate stories. One agent recalled the story of a conversation he'd had when his father was on his deathbed. A woman shared the story of a miscarriage that no one knew she'd had. I was amazed by how many people confessed that they were afraid to speak in public. I'd encourage them: "Talk to us. Tell us something. Anything." After they'd spoken they'd inevitably get applause. The room was incredibly nurturing and supportive.

Sometimes people were able to mend differences between themselves. One person revealed that she'd been terribly hurt by a colleague who was also in the room—and she mentioned his name. "No one here knows this, because I've kept it inside, but you betrayed me on a confidence about a client and used it to get *your* client a job."

The other party now had a chance to understand, talk, and begin to heal the relationship.

One year, I went around the room and instead of asking questions, I told everyone what I thought was great about them.

An agent spoke up and said, "How can you do this? Most of us are nuts!"

"I don't focus on your weaknesses," I said, "I focus on your strengths. If I focused on your weaknesses, I'd jump out a third-floor window."

That got the laugh I'd hoped for, so I continued: "I look for something that's good and positive and then help you find a way to push that out front."

Although I was the leader, I also participated. I told the story of being punished for raking leaves, and about how angry I was at my father for whipping me when I'd done nothing wrong—but how understanding the situation had helped me learn to do what was necessary, even though I didn't like it. Once I told the story of my birth and how my mother had almost lost me. By sharing my vulnerabilities, I was able to motivate others to share theirs.

In January of 2000, our meeting was about epiphanies. I chose the topic because I had recently experienced an epiphany, a spiritual flash that would change the way I viewed myself.

As 1999 ended, I was really concerned that the Y2K fears were authentic and that something terrible would happen as December 31, 1999 became January 1, 2000. I thought I wouldn't be able to use an ATM or go to the bank, so to calm myself, I hid thousands of dollars of cash in the house. I hid the money in different drawers in my closet and in a secret box that looked like a Bible but had the center cut out. I put some in the safe. I stored as many five-gallon bottles of water on my property as I could get. I worried about our computer systems. I was so nervous that it had become a joke among my friends that if something bad happened, they could just go to Sam's house. No kidding.

That's when I had my epiphany, obviously related to my fear of Y2K: If we love someone, it is important to tell them, and to tell them *why* we love them. I could not go to my grave—whether Y2K struck that month or forty years later—without sharing my feelings with those I cared most deeply about. So as the year drew to a close, I wrote two dozen letters to the most important people in my life. "I've been doing a lot of thinking as we approach the millennium," I wrote. "You are one of the people I truly love, and I want to tell you why."

I mailed them all weeks before January 1, 2000, because I didn't know if the mail would be delivered afterward.

The response was amazing. People said, "I knew you loved me, but I didn't know just how much. This means more to me than you'll ever know."

When I came back to work on the first Tuesday of January 2000—with a little humor and perspective in hand, and relieved that disaster had not occurred—I knew I had to reveal myself and tell my crazy story at the first meeting of the new millennium. I said, "I had an epiphany during the holidays: I needed to tell people that I loved them and why." Some of the people in the room had gotten letters; to their credit, they didn't identify themselves as among the twenty-four, because obviously not everyone in the room had been included.

Then I went around that room and told each person something about them that I loved. I got through a hundred people in an hour and a half. For the next two and a half hours, people shared their epiphanies, and what they meant. This was probably the most incredible and emotional session I ever conducted.

Oh, and since we'd made it to 2000, I could finally give away all the water bottles.

———

I don't think my promise to my mother to always seek understanding ever came in more handy than when I got the opportunity at William Morris to broker two of the biggest TV sitcom deals ever. They were the most important accomplishments of my professional career, and definitive lessons in how money can challenge character.

By 1990, I had been the NBC packager for three years. I'd

sold a lot of pilots. A few had made it on air. But suddenly I was on the brink of packaging a show that I strongly felt had the potential to be important, and I was quite emotionally invested.

My friend Lee Cohen at William Morris represented two producer-writers: Andy and Susan Borowitz. They had worked on shows like *The Facts of Life* and *Family Ties,* and had a deal at NBC to write pilots.

A couple of agents in our New York office had signed the young rapper Will Smith and his partner, DJ Jazzy Jeff. I felt that Will Smith would be a big star. His music had already made a tremendous impact on kids all over the country. Brandon Tartikoff, at NBC, was smart enough to realize that this might bring a young demographic to his network. They'd already been successful with *Cheers* and *Family Ties,* but he needed something for Monday night.

Once NBC knew that Will Smith was interested in doing TV, I met with Lee Cohen and the Borowitzes and said, "Let's do a little pilot presentation." It was already too late to do a full-blown pilot because most TV pilots were ordered in December or January, produced in March, maybe April, and shown to potential advertisers in New York in May. This was the middle of March. The Borowitzes were already producing and writing another pilot for NBC, entitled *Have a Nice Day.*

Will Smith was game. Based on the real-life experiences of producer/manager Benny Medina, the Borowitzes came up with a great fish-out-of-water idea: moving a young man from Philadelphia to Bel Air to live with his aunt and uncle in a home that reflected the best of the upscale African-American family style portrayed by *The Cosby Show.* The result shakes up everyone's lives both at home and at school.

From a social point of view, the series would follow in the Cosby tradition by showing a different—and nonstereotyped— side of the African-American community.

With Quincy Jones as executive producer and Benny Medina, James Lassiter, and Jeff Pollack as producers (they were attached to Will Smith through his music career), the Borowitzes as executive producers/writers/creators, and my client Debbie Allen as the director, we put the small pilot presentation together very, very quickly. Brandon Tartikoff called me every day, because he had begun to get excited.

Unfortunately, as we neared completion of preproduction, the participants' deals still weren't closed. It's the same old Hollywood story.

Will Smith, though unknown in the television market, had won a Grammy. The Borowitzes, who created the show, had certain financial aspects to their deal, certain controls, that they were not going to give up. We also had a deal with NBC Productions to be the studio that made the show. Although NBC owned the "studio" that would produce *The Fresh Prince of Bel-Air,* and NBC would make money from selling advertising, the "studio" wanted a bigger piece of the potential profits to pay for making the show. This created a problem. There's never more than 100 percent to divvy up, and no one would budge.

To complicate matters personally, on April 3, Mary and I had planned to hold a huge birthday party at our house for Sam, who was turning two. It just so happened that the Borowitzes and their daughter would be there, as would Debbie Allen and her children, many of my NBC friends, plus several of our other personal friends. We had a pony and a petting zoo, a clown, and all the usual birthday stuff.

The day before the party, everything blew up. We were supposed to film the show the following week, but we could not close everyone's deals. If the 2007–2008 writers' strike has taught us anything, it's that everyone negotiates not for today, but for tomorrow. Everyone involved wanted to make sure that if this was a success they'd get a bigger piece of the pie.

And I'd been given an ultimatum: "You either save it or drop it." The Borowitzes were happy to let it go and focus on their other pilot. (*Have a Nice Day* was *Family Ties* set in 1973, and it looked like a winner.) Everybody was getting upset and angry.

By the time people started ringing the doorbell for the birthday party, I'd been up all night trying to put together little Sam's new teeter-totter. I hadn't even showered.

When the Borowitzes arrived I took Andy aside and said, "This is worth saving." He agreed, but no one knew how to do it.

Moments later, the phone rang. It was Brandon Tartikoff and John Agoglia. They said, "So? What are we doing?" My instinct said that these important executives would not have called me at home on a Saturday if they wanted to let the show go. There was still life in the project—if we could find a way to compromise.

Andy said, "Don't these people know what's going on here?" He meant the birthday party and family time. I said, "You know what? We want this to happen, and we've got to figure it out, together."

I had to take the lead. I couldn't let it die. The show had success written all over it. Despite the party, I knew it was now or never—especially since I had most of the people involved right there at the house!

Within thirty minutes, I had the Borowitzes, Debbie Allen, and Leslie Lurie (the VP of comedy development at NBC) on the phone with Brandon Tartikoff. We gathered in Sam's nursery. Every portable phone in the house was taken. Outside, the party went on full blast.

Debbie Allen kept driving the creative and social aspects: "This is going to be a hit. It's time for this in the African-American community. This is the next *Cosby Show*."

The Borowitzes chimed in about creative directions in which they could take the show.

Leslie Lurie told Brandon, "I can put a lot of shows on the air for you, but this is the one that I know will go all the way."

I kept saying we needed to compromise in order to be winners in success. We all had to give up something.

Will Smith wasn't on the call, but he was near his phone. He didn't have any issues, other than his agents holding out for a little more profit participation and a little more money.

We talked for two hours. Debbie Allen's nanny had taken care of Debbie's children as well as the Borowitz's daughter. The party had ended, and Mary took young Sam and Mary Lane to the mall. In the end it came down to Quincy Jones, the Borowitzes, and NBC Productions figuring out how to split the valuable back-end ownership percentages. And we knew that paying Will Smith a little more, so he felt like the Grammy-winning star he was, wouldn't hurt either.

The situation resolved itself when we all put aside being stuck on our personal agendas and tried to understand the other points of view. What if we were in the other guy's shoes? What would we have wanted? Then, thinking of the overall greater good, we all realized that if we just gave ourselves the opportunity to create this world of *The Fresh Prince of Bel-Air,* everyone would benefit—and that without the show no one would get anything.

———

The second of the two sitcoms with a story I want to share is *Everybody Loves Raymond,* and it took a lot of understanding to keep it on the air when the original seven-year contract had expired and salary disputes arose.

Normally, as long as a TV series is successful enough to keep on the air, the original contracts specify that the actors and other principals are tied to the show for five to seven years, even if, with success, there are contract renegotiations and pay raises along the way. After that, the network typically has to pay a lot to retain everyone, often on a year-to-year basis.

After seven seasons, *Everybody Loves Raymond* was the most successful sitcom on CBS. Ray Romano had won a producing Emmy and an acting Emmy, Patty Heaton had won two acting Emmys, Doris Roberts three, and Brad Garrett two. Executive producer Phil Rosenthal and the show had won the Best Show Emmy. Tucker Cawley had won the Best Writer Emmy. (Only the late Peter Boyle had been overlooked, which upsets me still.) Obviously, CBS desperately wanted to keep the show on the schedule. Also, it could help launch some new shows, like *Two and a Half Men,* to eventually take its place. Which it did. And it is a big hit today and currently in negotiations to extend its run.

So the big question was: Would *Raymond* come back for an eighth season?

Ray and Phil Rosenthal had very strong feelings about going out on top. If they stayed, they wanted it to be exactly right both creatively and financially. Ray was my client, and together with his manager, Rory Rosegarten, and his lawyer, Jon Moonves, we negotiated Ray's deal, getting him a big piece of the income that would be generated when the show got syndicated to other stations after its first run on CBS. CAA renegotiated Phil's deal, with similar results.

Rory Rosegarten, Jon Moonves, and I had many discussions with Les Moonves, his number two Nancy Tellem, and Debbie Barak in CBS Business Affairs. We all met together and separately as we fought our way through the details. One day, Les, his brother Jon, and I met alone to try and settle the deal. We went around and around, and usually I was in the middle, trying to make peace. At one point, frustrated, Les said, "I'm done." He got up from the sofa, went to his desk across the room, and started answering e-mails. Jon, who understood his brother well, gave me a sign to just sit there quietly, which I did. Les was typing his e-mails—very slowly. After about five minutes, Jon broke the silence. "If we close Ray's deal, we'll be happy to give you some money for typing lessons." We all burst out laughing, and within days, after doing what was right for both sides, we closed the deal.

The rest of the cast were also nicely paid, but what they *really* wanted was to share in the syndication profits. After seven faithful and award-winning years, the cast felt that the powers that be should understand that their contribution to the show's success merited a percentage of the back end. The points were worth millions. Their request wasn't unprecedented. According to *Variety,* supporting actors on top-rated comedies—including *Friends, Frasier,* and *The King of Queens* (which followed *Raymond* on Monday nights)—all share in their show's syndication profits. The *Raymond* cast was offered more salary instead. No one was happy.

These days you can pretty much figure that the producing studio will hold on to at least 50 percent of the profit points from a TV show. CBS and HBO Productions, who had made the deal for the series with David Letterman's Worldwide Pants production company, jointly shared that 50 percent. Costs take another few percent. That left between 35 and 50 percent to split among everybody else. The creator, the star (Ray), and the executive producer get theirs next, and a few points are given away to people in the first couple of seasons, because it gives them incentive to work for less money in case the show becomes a hit. Then those points become hugely valuable.

In the summer of 2003, on the first day of rehearsals for the first episode of the eighth season, nothing had been resolved. Patricia Heaton called in sick for a week; Doris Roberts and Peter Boyle called in sick and each missed a few days. Brad Garrett, who also wanted a raise, stayed away longest. Only Ray showed up every day. The show was canceled for the week, and slowly but surely the agents and managers started calling and repeating what they had said all along: The cast wanted a fair piece of the back end. They knew the show would live in syndication for decades, around the world, sometimes airing three times a day on a single channel, and they felt they deserved a small piece of a very large pie.

During the week that Peter Boyle had called in sick, Les Moonves ran into Peter and his wife, Lorraine, at Wolfgang Puck's Beverly Hills restaurant, Spago. Les walked up to the Boyles, and simply smiled and said, "Well, good evening," and without missing a beat, Peter responded—as only Peter could— by saying, "I'm feeling much better tonight."

Even though I was only Ray's agent, I believed the cast was right: Everyone needed to be rewarded for the show's success. Without Ray there'd be no show; with no cast, well . . . it was pretty much the same situation. Or at best it'd be a different show—and who can quantify how much this particular cast's chemistry contributed to the show's being a hit. Taking nothing away from anyone, it was a team effort.

To complicate matters for me, after seven years of working closely together, the other cast members had become my friends, and I believed it was my personal responsibility to privately help calm the storms if I could. I needed to call them—Doris, Patty, Peter, and Brad—and say, "Just go back to work." I knew Leslie Moonves would not reward them for staying away from the set. We may have had a long and strong friendship, but in this case Moonves was also the Godfather. You don't leverage the Godfather. He will be good as gold if you play by the rules, but if you try to screw or pressure him, he ain't gonna respond. The cast had to return to the set, if only provisionally. They had to have blind faith and trust that negotiations would continue on their behalf and that their return would not be construed as a surrender.

Not so easy in Hollywood, unless you're just starting out and have no alternative.

At times it seemed certain that the show could not survive. I would go to my church, Bel Air Presbyterian, and get on my knees like my mother told me to do, and pray to God, "Please give me the strength to soften everyone's hearts so that we can get this deal concluded."

I don't know how much praying goes on in Hollywood, but this situation required it. This was about doing the right thing. It was about more than just the cast. Hundreds of people whom I'd gotten to know over the years—the grips and the electricians, people in wardrobe, makeup, craft services, the writers, the directors—had cornered me when I visited the set as the seventh season wound down, asking, "Are we gonna be back next year? Do I need to look for another job?" And now that they were back, they had no idea if they'd be able to stay.

Finally, one night in Ray's dressing room, Ray took the initiative and suggested to Rory, Jon, and me that he should share some of his back-end profits with the cast. Not only did this show Ray's character, it demonstrated his leadership and how much he appreciated the cast. For them to know that Ray set the example, and that part of their compensation would come out of his pocket *first,* would make the whole situation feel right. Next, Les Moonves and CBS stepped up to share a piece of their syndication profits, and I arranged for the William Morris Agency to do the same. Phil Rosenthal joined us as well, and so did Lee Gabler at CAA, who shared the representation of the package with me and who represented David Letterman's company Worldwide Pants. Then one by one the remaining players stepped up to the plate and took a cut.

Together, everyone achieved more. Each of the cast members now had a piece of the back end. They'd also agreed to return to the show should it have a ninth season. Money challenged character and character won through understanding.

———

I have probably given more free advice since leaving William Morris than during my entire time there. I have joined boards and given back to friends who have helped me. I became president of the Duke of Edinburgh's Award Young Americans' Challenge at the invitation of HRH the Prince Edward. Ole Miss chancellor Robert Khayat and vice chancellor Gloria Kellum asked Mary and me to become two of four chairmen of the new Ole Miss Capital Campaign. Robert and Gloria also asked me to be cochairman of the advisory board of the Gertrude Ford Center for the Performing Arts at Ole Miss, along with Morgan Freeman. In addition, I became president of the Debbie Allen Dance Academy board, president of the Hollywood Radio and Television Society, and chairman of the TV Academy Hall of Fame, and I am currently on the board of the Eudora Welty Foundation and the National Committee for the Arts at the Kennedy Center in Washington, D.C.

Sometimes I should just say no, but I will do anything if I sense a need, and if my work is appreciated.

And then, I took on what turned out to be a full-time "volunteer" job—one that tested my ability to both understand and compromise daily.

Years ago, when I became an agent, I called Albert Marks, the chairman of the Miss America board of directors, who'd run the pageant for decades. I told him about my history with pageants, that my wife was a former Miss Mississippi, and that I was now an agent with William Morris in Beverly Hills. I told him to let me know if there was anything I could ever do to help. Turned out I could. He needed assistance booking hosts and judges for the telecasts, and help with any postpageant TV bookings that might include the current Miss America. For example, I helped Vanessa Williams get a Diet Coke commercial while she was Miss America 1984.

The Miss America Organization also invited me to help judge the pageant twice, in 1984 and 1986. Afterward, scores of state people called to ask me to judge *their* competitions. Miss Texas. Miss Oklahoma. Miss Tennessee. Miss Mississippi. I thought, Okay, maybe I can do this once. Instead I did it every summer for ten straight years, through 1996. The last contest, Miss Texas, had eighty entrants, and it just about killed me. You have to talk to each girl for ten minutes. It took days just to get through the interviews! After that, I decided not to judge anymore—but I still helped. With my William Morris partner, Jim Griffin, I negotiated to put Regis and Kathie Lee on the show as hosts when the pageant was on ABC. Also, I knew the ins and the outs of the pageant so well that I could talk any of the judges—who included Debbie Allen, Cicely Tyson, James Lipton, Phylicia Rashad, Joan Van Ark, and Delta Burke—through the process before they arrived in Atlantic City.

Fast-forward to early 2005: Four months after I'd left William Morris, I was eagerly anticipating having a chance to relax, play some golf, and lose twenty pounds.

Three Miss America board members—Ron Burkhardt and former Miss Americas Phyllis George and Donna Axum Whitworth—called me. ABC had dropped the pageant and needed someone to help make a new deal. Oh, and there was an opening on the Miss America board if I was interested. I said, "Deal, yes. Board, no." That is, until I said yes to joining the board.

First, I helped sell the pageant telecast to Country Music Television (CMT) for the 2006 and 2007 contests. Then, in February 2006, the Miss America board decided to toss out the sitting chairman and nominate me from the floor. I said, "No, no, I don't have time! I have to get back to what I'm doing! I've already helped you with CMT! I can't do this!"

I won the election 15 to 1. You know who voted against me? Me!

I reluctantly agreed to be chairman—though for only one year—because I understood why I'd been elected. (Naturally, as I write this, I'm going into my fourth year.) I had experience working with nonprofit organizations, I had established and worked with various scholarship organizations, and obviously, I knew a lot about television. How could I not help out an organization that is the single largest source of scholarship for young women in the *world*? Besides, I got to work with some of my favorite people: former Miss Americas Rebecca King Dreman, who served as my vice chairman, Donna Axum Whitworth, and Phyllis George; *Newsweek*'s Tammy Haddad; and Las Vegas philanthropist Lynn Weidner. These women, and Mary, were truly the source of my strength during the rebuilding of the Miss America brand.

When I accepted the job, I knew that my willingness to understand everyone's point of view would be tested at every moment. I had to reinvigorate an aging brand despite resistance from an entrenched system and people who had done things their way for a long time. Art McMaster, the president and CEO of Miss America, had done the best he could in running the organization, but he had no one to help him with network relationships, potential sponsorships, and proper evaluation of staff, as well as with the local and state pageants. I'm sure I made Art and his staff nervous, but I was determined to take my responsibility seriously and "polish" what had become a very tarnished crown.

I immediately discovered that we were almost bankrupt. I

told the board, "No more expenses. If you don't like it, resign. After all, we *are* a nonprofit." I also took no salary or expense reimbursements.

Art and I let half of the Atlantic City staff go, as difficult as that was, and made a deal with Robert Earl for the Planet Hollywood Hotel in Las Vegas to be the new home base for the televised finals. We persuaded the Children's Miracle Network to become our national platform partner to help support money-raising efforts to fund and secure our scholarship program. We also made sponsorship and marketing deals, and eventually went into the black for the first time in thirteen years.

The 2006 Pageant was CMT's highest-rated program in its twenty-four-year history. Everyone should have been happy. The 2007 Pageant also produced stellar ratings, but then CMT decided not to pick up our option. I couldn't believe it.

After the second CMT Pageant had aired, John Ferriter—our William Morris agent—and I spent from April to August of 2007 seeking out anybody at any network who could be begged into taking a meeting to talk about a deal with Robert Earl for the pageant. We got four offers, and in the end had to decide between the Hallmark Channel, which would have let us put on the pageant just as the organization had done for years, and Discovery/The Learning Channel, which wanted to update everything and also do a reality series about the girls leading up to the actual pageant finals.

"If you think about it, the Miss America Pageant was one of television's first 'reality' shows," I said in defense of the idea. "Now we have to catch up with the expectations of a young audience raised on reality TV, and still maintain the professionalism and decorum that's a hallmark of the show and scholarship program." I was willing to gamble losing some of the pageant's older audience to get a younger set of viewers.

Needless to say, the decision to try something new upset the traditionalists. I told the state directors, "If this reality series brings young people to the pageant, then we need to do it. If we want to survive, we have to attract a younger audience. We have to make young girls want to grow up and be Miss America."

———

The series, *Miss America: Reality Check,* ran for four weeks leading up to the pageant finals in January 2008. The results had no bearing on who won the crown, but it introduced the girls to America and revealed that they were real women, not just perfect bodies in swimsuits and evening gowns. And, more important, more than twenty million people witnessed the crowning of Miss Michigan, Kirsten Haglund, as Miss America 2008.

The reality show truly expanded the way in which America thought of the pageant contestants and Miss America in general. The girls discussed gay marriage, abortion, and more. One nineteen-year-old said, "My parents got pregnant with me at their high school prom." (Her parents would be in the theater when their daughter competed.) "If my parents had aborted me," she said, "I wouldn't be here. But I am, and they're still together . . . and they are so proud of me."

When I watched a rough cut of the first episode, I was shocked to hear one of the reality show consultants actually ask Miss Alaska, "Are you a virgin?"

It was okay to discuss virginity, but why make it so personal? I thought, Why is this important? Do viewers want to know that about her? Nonetheless, Miss Alaska answered the question brilliantly, without actually answering it. She said that we shouldn't judge people by certain prescribed standards. We should look inside them, at their hearts, and ask what kind of person they are.

When the first installment of the reality show was edited together, I wanted to watch the rough cut and get a variety of reactions, so my whole family watched with me. Talk about diversity of opinion. Mary and I both felt that the show wasn't as uncomfortable as we thought it could have been. Mary Lane said, "These girls signed up to do their swimsuit, talent, and evening gown—not to do a relay race, climb out on a rope, or dive into a pool if they answer a question incorrectly."

(I suddenly remembered Mary, as Miss Mississippi, pillow-fighting over a mud pit!)

Young Sam loved it. He thought it was awesome. "I never knew these Miss America girls were so cool," he said.

Ah, the meaning of "to each his own." I'm not complaining. My own household has always reflected a great sampling of public opinion. And, as in any family, it always helps to understand and accept one another's points of view if you want to get along.

————

The Wednesday of Pageant Week 2008, in Las Vegas, I walked into the state executive director meeting. I could tell that some people had seen the reality show and appreciated what I'd tried to achieve by taking the show to TLC. I looked into the eyes of supporters like Briggs Hopson, Dewana Little, Shelley Taylor, Amalia Schwerdtmann, and Joe and Gail Sanders and knew that I was doing the right thing. But the horrified looks on many faces in the audience told me I had a lot of work to do to make those who thought I was Darth Vader understand the reality of our situation.

"I know what every single one of you thinks about the reality show," I said.

The room fell silent. "Those of you who liked it have told me personally. Those of you who don't have told someone else who has told me personally. So I know what every single one of you thinks."

The crowd was speechless.

How did I know? I'd been told to read the unofficial online

message boards for the Miss America Pageant. Here's what I discovered: There were several attacks on my character and integrity. They were saying that I had overplayed my hand, that I was killing the Miss America program.

You know what they say: "No good deed goes unpunished."

A lot of attacks were very personal. I had no idea people could be so cruel, but anonymity allows the venom to spew. All I could do was let those comments roll off my back, and move forward.

"I don't care what you think of me," I continued. "I know change is hard. That's why I sent every one of your girls a book by one of my favorite authors, Dr. Spencer Johnson, called *Who Moved My Cheese?* It's about the effects of change in your life, and how change is good.

"Many of the young ladies sent me beautiful thank-you notes because the book spoke to the changes in their own lives and their participation in the changes in the Miss America tradition. They told the judges in their interviews that they embraced this change. So either they're lying, or you're not communicating. The girls get it; you'd better be getting it too, because this train has left the station! Just like you, I am also a volunteer. I am doing this because I believe in the Miss America program."

My finding that common ground helped us turn the corner. Afterward, many of those in the audience came forward to pledge their support. "We get it, and we're totally ready to embrace the change." I felt vindicated.

———

I *do* believe in Miss America because, despite all the politics and personalities and unanticipated problems I encountered trying to set right a program in transition, it really all comes down to the young ladies of fine character who travel the long road from their communities to that pageant stage, and the state delegations who support them. Some of those state volunteers were the very first to stand up and support my new vision for Miss America, and I will always appreciate them.

Perhaps one of the most touching moments of the 2008 Pageant Week illustrates this best. One day, I watched Miss Vermont, Rachel Ann Cole, rehearse her talent segment. After the rehearsal each girl meets with her state delegation to get critiques and encouragement. Rachel was all alone—no one from her state organization had come. She looked so sad. I was about to talk with her when I was pulled into a press conference. I made a mental note to find her afterward. But when I came back, she was wearing a big smile. I said, "Rachel, are you okay?"

"Something wonderful happened," she said. "I have no one here. So after my talent rehearsal, the Florida delegation took me in and gave me their critique. I made some adjustments that I feel really good about. They made me feel like my mother was here."

I told the story later that week at the Miss America Breakfast. Afterward, eight hundred people applauded and Mary Sullivan, the executive director for Florida, got a standing ovation. All I could say—and I knew this in my heart from a lifetime's experience—was this: "Never forget. Everybody needs a mother." My mother believed that understanding how others feel, or how they might react to any given situation, could identify a road map to happiness. Like Mary Sullivan, my mother always had a knack for discovering if she was needed, and then worked hard to satisfy that need. It's a knack I try to execute every day of my life!

SEVEN

Family Matters: It Takes a Good Parent to Make a Good Child

We all need someone in our lives who thinks we are special or perfect or wonderful or talented or handsome or beautiful. We need someone who accepts us and even celebrates us for who we are. No one on their deathbed ever said, "My parents were too nice to me. They told me they loved me too often."

A good child's job is to be obedient and courteous. Even though I got different messages from each of my parents about how to act, how to think about my place in the world, and what was expected of me, I tried to please them both. I tried to behave respectfully.

A good parent's job is much more complicated. Anyone who has raised a child knows that parenting requires a great deal of patience and wisdom, trial and error, and, especially, love.

A good parent loves his child unconditionally. She knows and understands her children's strengths and weaknesses, and tries to focus them on the former, and on using those strengths to work on their weaknesses, where they can. But the weaknesses aren't emphasized or made to be the most important thing. A good parent would never simply say to a child, "You need to work on this," without also acknowledging how well they've done in some other area. If a parent helps a child develop his or her strengths, the child will eventually realize, from a position of confidence, that he or she can succeed in other areas that require improvement.

But how do you become a good parent? Is there a course you can take? There should be. Otherwise, I think it starts with having been parented well.

———

My mother loved me, Jamie, and Billy with relentless cheer and commitment. She would come into our rooms every morning singing, "When the red red robin comes bob bob bobbin' along, along, there'll be no more cryin' and no more sighin', as he sings a song, wake up, wake up, you sleepy heads, get up, get up, get out of bed, cheer up, cheer up, the sun is red, live . . . love . . . laugh and be happy." She was excited when we trudged home from school each afternoon and always had our favorite snacks waiting. And, as night fell, she was always optimistic about the wonders the next day would hold. If any—or all—of us kids had an overnight guest, she'd conjure up some popcorn or Rice Krispies Treats and we'd all watch scary movies together.

Momma massaged our aching muscles when we started playing sports, and cooked us our favorite meals every day. She loved us through the disappointments, and taught us the lessons that she thought would help us as we grew.

When we needed discipline, Momma rarely spanked us, but she would stand us in the corner "until you know how to act." Usually, we'd all be in three different corners at the same time. Later, when we'd grown up, she'd remember those moments and laugh, saying, "It didn't take more than five minutes before I'd hear three voices chirping, 'I know how to act, I know how to act.'"

Momma also made sure we were involved in every aspect of the First Baptist Church, from Sunday school to Wednesday prayer meeting to children's choir. When we were old enough, we got to go to the "big church" and hear the preacher's sermons.

My mother's cooking also played a big part in our lives. Anyone from the South knows that food is at the heart and soul of most every activity and part of the rituals that honor character, mark victories, encourage hope. My mother cooked special meals and desserts to reward my brothers and me for getting good grades, excelling in sports, winning school elections, and "doing the right thing." She made the most incredible fried chicken, fried pork chops, fried okra and squash, mashed potatoes, purple hull peas and onions, western beans, corn bread, etc. Aunt Betty made the same recipes; they got them from their mother, Grandmother Kirkpatrick.

When I was a boy, my mother made three meals a day, every day. We went out to eat only on the rare special occasion, and it was usually to a restaurant called Donald's in Nettleton for the best steak and onion rings I've ever tasted. Later in life, a home-cooked expression of love was among the best gifts I could receive. Dolly Parton made me biscuits and gravy and fried chicken. Pearl Bailey made me roast chicken and collard greens. Kathie Lee Gifford whipped up enchiladas and guacamole. My client David Trainer's wife, Deborah, made the most awesome peach pie I've ever tasted, and gave me one after almost every deal I closed for David to direct a TV show (*Designing Women*, *That '70s Show*).

Give me that pie over a bottle of Cristal, or a weekend at a luxury resort, any day.

———

In contrast, my father loved his boys as much as he could love anyone, but he had less means by which to express it—and less time. He traveled often as a clothing salesman, and on those rare weekends that he did come home, he would be at the coffee shop on Saturday and Sunday mornings with his friends, or on the golf course. He never went to church with us. In fact, his refusal to attend was the reason for some of the earliest arguments I remember my parents having. But to his credit, he allowed my mother to take the lead in our spiritual education.

My father could also get angry in a split second over the most ridiculous things. He insisted that, if our rear ends were not on the seats of our bikes, the bikes be put in the garage, even if we had just dropped them in the backyard long enough to have lunch. Sometimes my father asked us to caddy at the golf course for him and his friends. But that "honor" came with strict rules. For instance, we weren't allowed to talk, or even whisper, during the game. If we did, he would yell or threaten to whip us right then and there. Once, back at the clubhouse after a game, I asked my father if he thought deaf mutes made the best caddies. He never let me caddy again. I guess that was my answer!

If Jamie, Billy, and I got into fights, he'd make us put on boxing gloves and duke it out. I hated that so much. Daddy spanked us with his hand, or whipped us with his belt, whenever he felt we needed it. I think it hurt him to do so, since he would always come to our rooms to apologize afterward—but it continued until our early teens. We were afraid of him in more than the typical "Wait until your father gets home" way (something my mother never said), and I did everything that I could to keep my mouth shut and steer clear of any trouble.

I found out early on that my father would be happy if I made good grades or accomplished something he could brag about. Naturally, I tried hard to please him. But Momma warned us not to tell him our problems. "He's not good at handling problems," she'd say. So we took them to her, and usually he never knew.

With my father often gone, I needed positive male role models to emulate. Fortunately, I found them, or my mother found them for me.

David Williams, my Boy Scout leader, had been a star athlete in high school. He understood exactly what it took to not only engage but inspire the spirits of the young men in our community. His wife, Elnor, was one of my adopted mothers and his son, Lee, was one of my best friends. His daughter, Lara, was the prettiest girl in Amory. To be honest, we were all a little afraid of Mr. Williams; he could be tough as nails. But I found out that he also had a warm heart. When I worked on my music merit badge, I had to memorize a song on the piano, and then play it at a Scout meeting. I played "Danny Boy," and afterward Mr. Williams asked me to stay behind. He told me that I had no way of knowing this, but "Danny Boy" was his favorite song. He asked me if I could also sing it for him while I played it on the piano, and I said, "Yes sir, pull up a chair." After I finished Mr. Williams had tears in his eyes. Later that year, I won the Scoutmaster's Award as the most outstanding Scout in Troop 36. And guess who snuck into the back of the Scout Hut to see me win that award . . . my father. I was so thrilled.

Paul Thompson was the Boy Scout leader who took me to the Philmont Scout Ranch in Cimarron, New Mexico, when I was thirteen years old, and to the National Boy Scout Jamboree in Farragut State Park in Idaho the next year as one of the Mississippi delegates. At the Jamboree, Mr. Thompson, who was also a Mississippi highway patrolman, made me the troop correspondent. My job was to write articles about all the boys in our group. I also got to meet and interview Vice President Spiro Agnew, Olympian Jesse Owens, and world welterweight and middleweight boxing champion Sugar Ray Robinson—all of whom attended the Jamboree. I mailed articles to every newspaper in

Mississippi. At the end, I was chosen as one of the top three Scout correspondents in the nation. I won a Smith-Corona typewriter with the Boy Scout insignia on it. It's still in my garage.

Another role model was my high school football coach, Earl Stevens. I hated football, but wanted to please him. I also babysat his kids and taught them to swim. My senior year, Coach Stevens nominated me for All-Conference Tackle. Through his mentoring and support, I had become a fairly good football player. When I was ready to leave Amory and go to Los Angeles, his great gift to me, as you know, was a loan to help make it possible.

I also learned a lot from my pastor, the Reverend Larry Kennedy, at the First Baptist Church. He came to Amory from Louisiana when I was a freshmen in high school. He didn't know anybody, so I told him about everyone at church. He put me on the Search Committee to help find a new music minister. Reverend Kennedy was young and vital, and would come to all our football games. He was part of our youth group and would take us on retreats. He later became president of William Carey College in Hattiesburg, Mississippi. Sadly, he's passed away.

Years later, my father-in-law, Bob Donnelly, became a great influence on me as well. Originally from Chicago, he had swept my mother-in-law, Shirley Bragg, off her feet at the end of World War II. Shirley was a gorgeous Southern belle from Decatur, Alabama. They married in 1945, when Shirley was nineteen and Bob was thirty. Bob was strong, kind, extremely patient, and certain about what was right. For instance, when I turned forty, Bob bought me a pair of white-buck shoes. "Sam," he said, "all well-dressed men over forty *must* have a pair of white bucks." I still have those shoes and I think of Bob every time I wear them.

I also admire the relationship that Bob and Shirley shared for almost sixty years. They loved and supported each other beautifully, and set an example for Mary and me that has stayed with us throughout our twenty-seven-year marriage. I sometimes wish my parents could have been as happy as Bob and Shirley, but I guess it wasn't meant to be.

———

In the absence of my father's having a steady presence in my life, I was always more than happy to have what felt like a second mother: my aunt Betty. She was the most positive, confident, and funny person I knew. In fact, as a child I never saw my aunt Betty cry. She was more of an extrovert than Momma, who was kind of shy in public. But in private, they would tell stories about their childhoods, their friends, and our grandparents—Nanny and Granddaddy—and would laugh so hard it was contagious. Momma and Aunt Betty's favorite family story was about their distant cousin, Lex Humphries, on their mother's side of the family. They could not hold back the laughter at the very mention of his name. Apparently, Lex had jumped off the roof of the old three-story high school building holding an umbrella as a parachute! He broke both of his legs and walked with a limp for the rest of his life. Between giggles, Grandmother Kirkpatrick would "shush" them, saying, "Never let anyone know that Lex is kin to us." All of us kids got so much joy watching Momma and Aunt Betty laughing together. I was so happy anytime that Momma would pile us all into her red Mercury convertible and say, "Let's go to Aunt Betty's house and see what [her children] Dan and Mary are up to."

Aunt Betty is like my momma in so many ways. She always had great snacks waiting for us, and she was always interested in what we did at school, who our friends were, and what our goals were. I loved being with Aunt Betty. Often, I'd ride my bike to her house just to sit on her sofa, have a Coke, and talk to her about whatever was on my young mind. Even after I went away to college, one of the first things I'd do when I came back to

Amory for the holidays was to go to Aunt Betty's for a Coke and some conversation. In some ways, it was easier to tell her what was in my heart than to tell my mother. I'm not sure why, but it was.

There has never been a time in my life that Aunt Betty and her husband, Uncle Hal, have not influenced me. They are my children Sam and Mary Lane's Mississippi grandparents, and not a single Halloween, Christmas, Valentine's Day, Easter, or birthday passes without the kids getting a special card or note from *their* "Nanny and Pappy." I love my aunt Betty so much because I know how much she loves me!

———

My mother believed that good children come from good parents. Whenever she saw a boy or girl misbehave, my mother would say, "I wonder what his or her parents are like?" She knew that was important because she knew that children notice everything, then reflect it in their own behavior. Had she lived long enough, I know Momma would have been amazed to hear her wisdom expressed in the Stephen Sondheim musical *Into the Woods*, which opened on Broadway six months after she died. In the number "Children Will Listen," Bernadette Peters, who played the Witch, sang, "Careful the things you say, children will listen. Careful the things you do, children will see."

I know that my mother always tried to be a great role model for me, and I hope that my life honors her example. She was a wonderful parent. In fact, as painful as it was for our family to watch such a wonderful woman suffer and then pass away, she remained a devoted parent even at the end.

In August 1986 my mother fell ill and was rushed to the hospital, where it turned out that a diagnosis she had received the year before had been totally wrong. Now, a cancerous tumor the size of a grapefruit had punctured her stomach lining, and the doctors in Amory barely saved her from hemorrhaging to death.

When Aunt Betty called me, I flew from Los Angeles to my mother's bedside. The doctors told me about the cancer. I called my mother's ob-gyn, Dr. Richard Hollis (my friend Randy's dad), who told me that if this were his wife, he would take her to the M. D. Anderson Cancer Center in Houston, Texas.

We had to move quickly, and luckily a longtime friend of my mother's, Tommy Longnecker, had a private jet and was willing to let us use it. Tommy's pilot, a lovely man named Jimmy Vaughn, flew Uncle Hal, Momma, and me to Houston within hours of her diagnosis. Aunt Betty and Mary followed soon thereafter, along with several other relatives, including my in-laws, Bob and Shirley Donnelly.

My mother had extensive internal surgery two days later.

The surgeon, Dr. Richard Martin, looked exhausted when he came out of the operating room. He said they'd removed just about every organ that she didn't need to live. He told us he'd done the best he could, but that he feared that after the tumor had torn through the stomach wall, every organ in her body had been exposed to the cancer, which had already spread to her lymph glands.

I was devastated. Aunt Betty, Mary, and I tried to be strong for one another, but we couldn't help but break down and cry our eyes out. Over and over I asked myself why God would let this happen to this wonderful, perfect lady. I was almost angry. If her death was inevitable, I hoped he at least wouldn't let her suffer.

I asked Dr. Martin how long my mother had to live, and he told me that the best-case scenario would be six months. Chemotherapy and radiation might buy another three months at most. I'd seen friends' parents who had literally been burnt up by those treatments. I thought it would be better to have Momma normal and healthy for three to four months, and then terribly sick for two months, than to have her terribly sick and losing her hair for eight months. Aunt Betty agreed with me. But it had to be Momma's decision.

She agreed with us. The way she chose to die revealed great strength and a great understanding that life was meant to be lived to the fullest before going to a better place. I, on the other hand, felt absolutely helpless. It was a strange and terrible feeling: I'd accumulated a high level of power and influence in business, but now had to accept that I had no power over life and death. Still, I had to be strong just like my mother had been when my father, brothers, and I had been in the car crash. Now, the woman who had always helped everyone else needed help herself.

After she was released from the hospital in mid-October, we took Momma back to Amory and made arrangements for her care, including hiring a lovely man named Don Comer to live with her and bringing in Girlene Weaver, the night nurse who had helped Grandmother Kirkpatrick twenty years earlier. Mary and I flew to see her as often as possible, but couldn't be there as much as we wanted to be.

With several months ahead before she would be permanently bedridden, my mother worked hard to maintain a sunny disposition and set about saying her good-byes and putting her affairs in order. But most important, she had one more Christmas to plan, and it was going to be the biggest and best the family ever had.

My mother had always loved Christmas. She usually started celebrating at Thanksgiving and didn't stop until the New Year. She was always in the kitchen making our favorite Christmas cookies, divinity, fudge, cakes, and pies. One year she and I even reconstructed a Christmas Castle we'd seen in *Good Housekeeping* magazine—it took an entire weekend to make it out of cake and candy, and it served as the centerpiece at our Christmas dinner that year.

The entire family came to Amory for what would be Momma's last Christmas; even my high school English teacher was there. Although she had gotten thinner, my mother did her best to look as normal as possible for my brothers, Jamie and Billy, so that they didn't worry too much. In fact, my brothers had a hard time believing that she was dying—not in small part due to our father, who, in the aftermath of the divorce and the battle for our affections, did everything he could to make my brothers think that Momma wasn't really dying. In his words, it was "just a ploy that Sam and your mother concocted to get you to spend more time with her." That left me angry and speechless, but I decided to devote my energy to attending to my mother; I'd deal with my father later. Meanwhile, Momma just put on her best face so that Jamie and Billy would have something positive to remember her by.

Our Christmas celebration went on as it always did: a tree with lights blazing in many colors, Christmas Eve dinner at our house, and lunch the next day at Aunt Betty's. Momma also reinstated our long-standing personal tradition of my telling her what I'd learned during the year and describing my plans for the future.

By late February, the cancer had reappeared and her descent had begun. Mary or I went to Mississippi every single weekend starting in mid-February. For four weekends in a row, Aunt Betty called to tell me that Momma was in her final hours, but then Momma would rally by the time Mary and I got off the plane.

On one of those weekends, my mother said something not only unexpected but unimaginable: "I wonder how my life would have been different if I had married Warren Nasiff."

"Who's Warren Nasiff?" I asked. I vaguely remembered her mentioning the name to me as a child.

She said, "Do you remember me telling you about Frank Johnson?"

I did. He was her first husband, the doctor from Mobile, Alabama. Their marriage had been short-lived. That's where I had heard the name, and now she was finally telling me about Warren Nasiff. But why? Did she regret her life with my father?

My mother knew me well. Without my even asking, she answered the question. "But if I had married Warren, then I wouldn't have had you."

All of a sudden, I felt like George Bailey, in his darkest moment, wondering what the world would have been like if he had never been born. Later, I asked Evelyn Murch, an old nursing school friend of my mother's, about Warren Nasiff. "He was just the finest man you could have ever met, and he did everything he could to convince your mother to marry him," she explained. "He became a research physicist. He married and had a whole bunch of kids, but he really loved your mother. However, she had convinced herself to marry Frank."

Yes, like any child, I wondered what my family's life would have been like had I never been born. But much more important to me was the rare and profound moment in which I got to see my mother as an individual, wholly apart from myself, with her own pains and joys and sacrifices. She may have regretted marrying my father, but her children were the greater reward that she believed more than balanced the scales. My respect for her willingness to stay committed to her chosen path despite hardships, and her ability to find joy in the darkest of places, grew even more as I came to understand her life from an adult perspective.

My mother had great pain during her final weeks. Once, as I held her hand at her bedside, with tears in my eyes, she looked at me with perfect clarity, even though her wasted body was racked with pain, and asked me to lean in close. Whispering in my ear, she said that she didn't want me to worry about her and that she didn't want me to cry for her, for very soon she would be in Heaven, without pain, standing in the light of God's grace.

The weekend of Easter 1987, Aunt Betty told me the doctors had said Momma would not last the night. I caught the first flight to Memphis on Good Friday. I arrived in Amory at 5 P.M. Momma had barely spoken a word for two days, and she was only semiconscious. Aunt Betty and I walked into her bedroom. She was paralyzed on one side of her body, but with her good arm she reached out slowly to put her hand on my cheek. She smiled and told me she loved me. Then she dozed off until our friend Barbara Thompson arrived at the house for a visit. Aunt Betty brought her into Momma's bedroom, where I was sitting. Barbara said, "Mary Nell, I've made Sam a banana pudding." Suddenly, my mother opened her eyes, turned her head, looked at Barbara, and said, "Thank you, Barbara, he loves that pudding so much." Then she drifted off again.

While I sat by my mother's bedside, her words made me think of how food had long been part of the way she had shown her children and entire family her love. Food had helped all of us celebrate life.

———

My mother fell into a coma that night. Many of her friends kept vigil at the house, and there was never a time when I appreciated their strength and character more, because I wasn't sure how much longer I could maintain my own. The stressful situation had made me question many of my assumptions about life. Call it a crisis of faith. I could not believe that this selfless woman would have her life snuffed out so brutally when she'd always been a good Christian, a good person, a good mother. How could God take her away from us *and* put her through this pain?

During these sad days my aunt Betty's strength really came through. She could have simply collapsed when my mother's diagnosis was announced, because she was not only Momma's sister but her best friend. They had shared their *entire* lives.

Whenever I felt sorry for myself, her example of strength and steadfast faith was incredibly inspirational. She went to my mother's house every day. She was on the phone with me every night giving me the updates. If it hadn't been for Aunt Betty—who never let herself cry until the end—I'm sure we'd all have fallen apart.

Meanwhile, my mother still would not let go. Her doctors became convinced that she was waiting for someone. And then it dawned on me: Jamie and Billy. They had come home during Christmas, and Billy had come home again in March, just as Mom's health started to deteriorate again. But neither of them had seen Momma since—at her worst. It had been their decision, influenced by my father, not to come.

On Easter Sunday evening, Mary was in the bedroom, rubbing cream on my mother's hands and arms. I sat by the bed with Aunt Betty, my cousins Mary Nan Hodo and Mary Rogers, and Coach Stevens's wife, Lazette. I knew that even if I'd been able to convince my brothers to come, they might not be able to get there in time. So I did what I believed was the right thing: I told my mother that they were in the room with us. I told Momma we all loved her very much. "It's okay, Momma . . . it's okay to go. . . . We're all here."

Within moments, a peaceful look came over her face and she took her last breath and murmured the word, "Momma." We knew that she had just entered Heaven, where she was met by her mother. I am absolutely sure that Nanny walked Momma right into Heaven and into the light of God's grace. At last her pain was gone, and she was at peace.

I don't have the words even now to describe how I felt then, but I know this much: My mother was a consistent force for good in my life, never forgetting that her greatest responsibility was to set an example for me and my brothers about not only how to live our lives, but how to always appreciate the blessing of life—and how to pass it on to the next generation. She single-handedly held our family together, and even in her most trying moments she was the perfect role model.

My father, as you've now gathered, wasn't. He had tried to control me, but couldn't. There were times when shadows of darkness surrounded him. I realized more and more that I never felt as complete as when I stood in my mother's light.

During their divorce, I took her side. My mother had my father brought to court to make sure that we were taken care of in the style that we had grown accustomed to, and he resented her for that. After one year of paying alimony and child support, he stopped, even though he could well afford it. I worked to help my mother with the house payments.

On the day of my mother's funeral, my father sent me a message: "It will be a cold day in Hell before I'll let you sell your mother's house and settle her estate." Death is cold, but this was colder. Then, a week later, my father and his wife sued my mother's estate, trying to claim ownership of her home and half the value of some land and property that her parents had left her. He had found a loophole in the divorce decree that gave him half the house. But because of his unwillingness to pay years of child support, we countersued.

From the moment I was notified of the lawsuit, I never spoke to my father again. And he wanted nothing to do with me. When his sister—my aunt Marilyn—and her husband, Uncle Bill, took my side as the battles continued, he refused to speak to them as well.

My father's behavior had been bad ever since the divorce, because I think he was consumed with guilt. There are many reasons for divorce, but one particular crossroads moment in my parents' marriage may be a metaphor for everything that followed. In the mid-sixties, my father was offered an opportunity to leave the clothing business, move to Los Angeles, and become a liquor distributor. My mother, however, adamantly objected. She did not want us to leave "Mayberry," she did not want us to leave her family in Amory, and she did not want my father in the liquor business, because she thought that it was evil and misguided.

They had a huge argument, and my father flew to Los Angeles anyway. He came back overwhelmed. He thought the traffic was bad. (This was in 1964; imagine if he could see it now.) So he gave in to my mother, but he remained resentful at what he decided was her attempt to spoil his dream, and anger festers. When, as an alternative, he suggested working for a liquor distribution company in Mississippi, she also opposed the idea. "I just can't let you do it to the boys or to me," she said.

My mother had a very pure vision of what the world should be. My father was probably more realistic, yet drawn to what my mother saw as "the dark side."

I remember my father saying to me, after the divorce, "I don't need a mother."

Imagine my surprise, then, when my youngest brother Billy, who remained close to our father, told me, "Dad's new wife— bosses him around; nothing he does is good enough."

Perhaps he traded one type of "mother" for another, but he'd made his choice.

———

It took me several years to settle the case. But four months after my mother's death, when Mary and I found out that we were to have our first child the next spring, I decided that my father should know that he was going to be a grandfather. As soon as he heard my voice, he hung up on me. Then, on January 20, 1988, one month before his fifty-ninth birthday, my father took his own life.

I have often reflected back on that moment, nine months to the day after my mother's death, and I can only imagine that my father woke up that morning, and in the purest moment of his life, looked Heavenward and said, "My God, what have I done?" Perhaps he was depressed over my mother's difficult death, and over his estrangement from his family, and just decided to end it then and there. After his funeral, I said to Mary, "If only Dad had been kinder during Momma's illness. If only he had tried to be there for me when I needed him most. He would have all of our attention now." His end was not what I would have wished for him, but confronted with the reality, I prayed that God would embrace him and allow him a final perfect peace.

———

My mother would have been a fantastic grandmother had she lived to meet Sam IV and Mary Lane, and it saddened me to know that she wouldn't be around to teach them the importance of the values and promises she believed led to a good life. I really wish she had known the kids, but more important, I wish they had known Momma.

Sam IV was born on Easter Sunday, April 3, 1988, a year after Momma passed. April 3 was also Grandmother Kirkpatrick's birthday. She had died when I was eight, and every year after that we went to the cemetery on her birthday to place flowers on her grave. Since my mother had died on Easter Sunday, I wondered if I'd ever be able to enjoy the holiday again.

Then, when Sam IV arrived one year later on both Easter Sunday *and* April 3, I remember thinking, Oh, Momma, I wish you could see this beautiful baby. Then I realized God was telling me, She knows.

But maybe she did meet Sam.

When Mary was seven months pregnant with Mary Lane, we had to fly through Dallas to get to Mississippi. Sam was thirteen months old, and I had to lug the stroller and car seat and diaper bag through the terminal. We had a ninety-minute layover. As we walked to the gate for the next flight, we saw a little old lady sitting in a wheelchair.

She looked about eighty-five, and wore a blue suit, exactly like the ones my mother wore. She wore a brooch like my mother's, and her hair was styled the same, only it was gray.

She looked like my mother would have looked had she lived another twenty-five years. I was astounded.

Sam had been really fussy, so we let him out of the stroller to burn off some energy. He ran right up to this lady and started patting her lap. She brushed his cheek and rubbed his hair and said he was beautiful.

When the flight attendant came to board the lady early, I asked Mary, "Who does that woman look like?"

"Oh my goodness," Mary said, understanding instantly.

On the plane we discovered that the woman in the wheelchair was seated right next to us. Mary was by the window; I held Sam in the middle; she was on the aisle.

During the flight, the woman—I never even got her name—took an apple from her purse, asked the flight attendant for a knife (you could have knives then), and cut tiny pieces off for Sam. My mother had always cut up apples for us when we were little. She'd even peeled them so we never had to eat the skin.

Sam crawled into the lady's lap and spent most of the hour-and-a-half flight there, letting her feed him this apple. He kept laughing, loving it. When it was time to land, we put Sam back in my lap.

At the gate, Mary took Sam by the hand and got him off the plane while I gathered all our stuff. Just then, the little old lady took my hand and said, "You have the most beautiful baby." I said, "Thank you." She said, "I was a nurse and used to take care of small children. I just want you to know—I see that your wife is quite pregnant—your new baby is going to be beautiful too." Then she said something that my mother always said: "Live every day to the fullest. You're going to have a wonderful life. God bless you."

My mother had told me all the time, "Live every day to the fullest."

As they wheeled the lady off the plane, I began to cry. I rushed into the terminal, baby paraphernalia in hand, hoping to catch her, but she wasn't there.

My mother had always told me that God can put an angel in our path for many reasons. An angel can come in the form of someone else, or can just be someone who steps into your path and makes you stop for a moment to prevent something bad from happening. I believe that I have a guardian angel who works full-time and sends me messages, usually in the form of a "lucky penny." Until that experience, my heart had been burdened. But afterward, I no longer felt any sadness about my mother's not knowing my children. Now I know she loves them as I would have wished for her to love them, and that love has only made me and Mary love our children more.

———

Being a parent myself has been . . . well: There are many words to describe the experience. Fascinating. Scary. Challenging. Joyful. Sometimes I find myself acting just like my mother, at other times like my father—which, frankly, surprises me. I spent my whole life making sure I wouldn't make the same parenting mistakes he did, but now I realize that there are some things you can't control. I believe that he must have really loved me, even when he wasn't any good at expressing it. I've come to realize that parenting is hard and requires being there for the children as often as possible. Unlike my mother's caution to my brothers and me, I *do* want my children to bring me their problems when they arise. But even now that my children are grown, I often realize just how much I still don't know. Talk about feeling one's way along in the dark. My mother-in-law, Shirley Donnelly, told me the night before Sam was born that "once this baby arrives, there won't be a moment free from worry. Is he crawling and walking on time? Who are his friends? Who is he dating? And after he marries and has children of his own, you'll worry about them as well!"

As usual, Shirley was right.

Of course, I worry and I love my kids so much that I don't want anything bad to ever happen to them. As every parent knows, that can make you more intrusive than you really want to be. After all, the whole idea of parenting is to teach the lessons, set the example, do the prep work, and let the kids go. We bring them up to leave us. When they do, it should make us proud—and it does—but it also causes anxiety and sadness. And so we hang in there to the point where, once our kids have become young adults, *they* have to let *you* know where the line is drawn.

My mother instinctively knew when to let me go off on my own. As my friend Jason Winters once told me, quoting Ralph Waldo Emerson (after Goethe): "Treat a man as he is and he will remain as he is. Treat a man the way he can be and should be and he will become as he can and should be."

Jason was absolutely right. I've always tried to pass it on.

Take my daughter, Mary Lane. She's a wonderful singer and actress and dancer, and is currently studying musical theater at NYU Tisch. In 2007, award-winning recording artist Michael Feinstein asked her to guest-star on the bill with him, Elaine Stritch, and Jason Graae, at Michael's "Standard Time" concert at Carnegie Hall. Michael and his partner, Terrence Flannery, have been dear friends for many years and were my clients at William Morris. They met Mary Lane when she was thirteen years old. Michael called her talented and engaging, and admired how she had so much knowledge at such a young age about all things Broadway. Mary has taken Mary Lane to New York at least twice a year since she was ten to see every show and every musical, and anything of import on the New York stage.

After Michael saw Mary Lane perform at her high school, in the lead role of Rosie in *Bye Bye Birdie,* he told me he thought she'd be a big star. A year later, he sang with her at a benefit in Mississippi.

Mary Lane was pretty relaxed about the whole Carnegie Hall appearance. I wasn't. I was nervous about her being properly prepared. She took her time choosing her music. I couldn't stop thinking about everything I imagined rode on her performance. I bugged her. She was nonchalant. Confident. That bugged me even more. I started asking, "When do you start rehearsing? When do you start memorizing? Have you called Michael this week?"

"I'll take care of it, Daddy," she said.

"No, Mary Lane," I said. "You need to learn it *right now.* We need to get the key set. When are you going to set the key? We've got to get you a rehearsal tape."

"Dad, I'll handle it," she said, as politely as possible.

I kept catching myself being intrusive just a split second too late.

Mary Lane wasn't as concerned about the singing part as she was about her hair and dress. She agonized about what she'd wear onstage. Mary and I flew into New York in October to take her shopping. But then she didn't seem happy with the dress we picked for her, and declared her independence. "I'm not going to wear the *ball gown* you picked," she said. "I want to wear something more in keeping with who I am."

Mary Lane would never have told us to just butt out, because she's not a disrespectful child. But I should have been more sensitive.

Of course, she was wonderful in the concert, and everyone raved about her talent, her hair—and the dress *she* chose.

———

Boys are, by nature, competitive with their fathers, and they want to be smarter and more successful than Dad. That's already happening to Sam IV, and I'm so proud of him. It took some painful personal work to realize that despite my strong desire for Sam to be an Eagle Scout or a Sigma Chi like me—now I understand even better why my father's wishes for me seemed so obviously right to him—it was not a requirement. He's interested in film, photography, and physical training—all great activities. And yet, like my dad, I've sometimes been too critical and fixated on my expectations, and I end up having to apologize to Sam. Once, when he came home from school and announced that he had made a 97 on a history exam, I asked, "Which questions did you miss?" Ouch! I should have just congratulated him on the great grade.

These days I can no longer say things like, "We're going to a nice event so why do you have to wear that knit cap?" Or "Why don't you brush your hair?" I did that when he was little. And the funny thing is, I discovered that when I don't criticize him, he's more peaceful, and sometimes surprises me by doing exactly what I'd want him to do—as long as I don't ask and try to force the issue. That's much better for all of us. My son is a great person—and his own man.

Unlike me, Sam doesn't care what anybody thinks of him. He will probably go through life with a lot less stress than I do. He is strong, free-thinking, confident, and totally capable. As early as the second grade, he showed a flair for thinking outside the box.

I'll never forget when he came home with an assignment for the annual "100th Day Project." Each child had to come up with a project using a hundred identical items. Most kids chose a hundred trading cards, or Band-Aids, or marbles, or packages of sugar, or photos of themselves. Sam . . . well, he wanted to catch a hundred snails and design a poster of a giant snail made up of the shells. Fortunately for him, our backyard was filled with all kinds of plants, and hundreds of snails. Sam got a bucket from the garage and went to work. Two hours later he brought his bucket of snails into the kitchen and explained to his mother and me that he now had to "de-slug" the snails he had collected so far.

"How are we going to kill them?" I asked.

"Just like you cook lobsters. We'll boil them."

And that's what we did, and Sam made the most incredible giant snail poster you've ever seen. He didn't even mind that some of the girls in his class screamed when he brought it in for show-and-tell.

―――――

As parents, we can easily go over the top trying to do everything for our kids. We know there's so much pressure out there to succeed socially and at school, and we often bring that pressure home. If our children don't do something quickly enough, we do it for them. If they don't understand what they're doing, we explain it for them. We want everything to go well, but we can end up hurting our kids because we're not allowing them to be responsible. We're not letting them understand the consequence of mistakes or giving them the chance to decide on their own that there must be a better way.

When I think about it, one reason I've been successful is *because* my mother allowed me the opportunity to fail. She believed, and let me know, that if I did fail, the experience would only serve to make me stronger. And, of course, if you can succeed when others suspect you'll fail, even a small success is a sweet, confidence-building experience.

The world today is a tougher, scarier, more challenging place than when I grew up, and I am predictably concerned about my children's futures. I want them to have wonderful, happy, productive lives, and not fail. Sometimes, because I've done well, I feel as if I can tell them how to do that, provide them with the practical steps. I try, but I've also realized that it can be a mistake. We can warn our kids about the potholes in the road, as they say, but we also have to give them the keys and let them drive down the road on their own.

———

Even before my kids entered kindergarten, I established Sunday night at our house as "Family Movie Night." By the time Mary Lane and Sam were in the third and fourth grades, they had already seen such classics as *Gone with the Wind, The Wizard of Oz, It's a Wonderful Life, The Sound of Music, Rear Window, The Ten Commandments, Anne of the Thousand Days, To Kill a Mockingbird, The Six Wives of Henry VIII, Raiders of the Lost Ark,* and every Disney movie known to man, especially *Mary Poppins,* over and over again!

Mary Lane loved the fantasy and romance, and Sam loved the movies with historical significance. Just like me, he was very interested in the history of England's royal family.

When Sam studied world history in the eighth grade, his teacher asked if anyone would like to answer a "really difficult" question for extra credit. "Who can name the six wives of Henry VIII?" Sam's hand shot up!

"*Can* you answer the question, Sam?" the teacher asked.

"Can I get double credit if I name the wives in order and tell you who their children were?"

The teacher, never figuring he could really answer the question, said, "Sure."

"Catherine of Aragon and her daughter Mary I. Anne Boleyn and her daughter Elizabeth I. Jane Seymour and her son Edward VI. Anne of Cleves, Catherine Howard, and Catherine Parr." Needless to say, Sam got the extra credit *and* made an A in the class!

Sometimes a "color within the lines" mentality is necessary, but sometimes it does not serve a child's creative nature. It's the person who can imagine life *outside* the lines, who truly can see a world full of possibilities, who will eventually discover happiness and success. As parents, we must embrace and encourage our kids' creativity, we must applaud their individuality. We must tell them that they are special. My mother taught me that, and it's one of her most valuable lessons—after all, you never know where the next person to change the world and make it a better place will come from.

———

Parenting, in its broadest sense, is not solely about helping our own children grow; it's part of how we deal with people outside the family as well. We can parent friends, and even other people's children who are friends of our children. I certainly "parented" agents at William Morris during the inspirational and motivational sessions I held.

I had also been parented there by the previous generation of senior agents like Tony Fantozzi, Jerry Katzman, Walter Zifkin, Norman Brokaw, Lou Weiss, and Larry Auerbach. Brokaw would probably go down in my book as having had the greatest impact on my career because he shared his clients, especially Bill Cosby; but more important, he shared his heart with me.

Fantozzi, Brokaw, and Zifkin were nurturers. The week before I got married, Fantozzi said, "I'm going to give you a little advice: When it comes to the house and the kids, if you're smart you'll just defer to her." (I think he actually said "smart goy," meaning non-Jew, but the advice is universal.) And that was that. I do have strong opinions, and Mary wants my opinion. But if she feels really strongly about something, then I defer to her. That was good advice. It's been a great relationship.

Lou Weiss, an agent and former chairman of the board who was at William Morris for over fifty-five years, gave me some fatherly advice that has forever served me well. "The best deal in Hollywood," he said, "is the deal where you have all the leverage in the world and you still leave a couple of dollars on the table. Why? Because you've planted the seed that will build a relationship based on character and decency. One day when you have no leverage at all, the person you made that deal with will remember how you treated him, and give you back those dollars that you once left on the table."

This works whether you're in show business or any other business. It works in life.

The longer I worked at William Morris, the more I found myself trying to pass on all I'd learned from those who had set the example for me. I learned how as I went along. You might call it management technique, but what is parenting anyway? Management with love.

Let's say one agent had really good communications skills but was terribly disorganized. And another had great organization skills but wasn't the most comfortable speaker. In public I'd recognize their strengths. In private, I'd say, "Your communications skills are so good you could sell ice cream to an Eskimo. I'm going to make sure that you're on the phone with the network, because you can really sell. But because you're so disorganized, we're going to have to talk to personnel and get you a really great secretary or trainee to help you organize your life.

You're not returning phone calls and you're not getting your paperwork done."

To the other, I'd reverse the facts. Often, I'd surprise both and make them a team.

———

In the end, parent and child, just as they are a family, are a team. The coach knows the road map to excellence and is a role model for the players. As my mother did, the coach supports them unconditionally and expects the same in return, as well as adherence to the rules of the game and the values of good sportsmanship. He utilizes each individual's strength and encourages work on their weaknesses. He may at times micromanage, but understands that the team is a living and breathing organism that must be allowed to learn from its mistakes and be flexible enough to respond to situations instinctively, because in the game, as in life, he can only teach, while the players must actually take the field. Afterward, he celebrates both team victories and individual achievements (even in defeat), and the cycle starts again, as it always must.

EIGHT

If You Can Walk with Kings…

If you can talk with crowds and keep your virtue,
Or walk with kings—nor lose the common touch,
If neither foes nor loving friends can hurt you;
If all men count with you, but none too much,
If you can fill the unforgiving minute
With sixty seconds' worth of distance run,
Yours is the Earth and everything that's in it,
And—which is more—you'll be a Man, my son!

—EXCERPT FROM "IF," BY RUDYARD KIPLING

When I was in the fifth grade, my teacher, Miss Harriet Nabors, gave us an assignment to learn twelve lines of a poem. At home, I riffled through the *Childcraft* books that came with our encyclopedia set. They were full of verse, fairy tales, adventure stories. I wanted to find a poem that ran *exactly* twelve lines. My mother said, "I think you need to learn this instead," and she turned to Rudyard Kipling's "If."

"Mom," I complained. "It's *thirty-two lines.*"

"It will come in handy someday," she said. "I promise!"

Truer words were never written. There are lines in "If" that describe the elements of good character and rule my life.

"If you can keep your head when all about you are losing theirs and blaming it on you." That was my life at William Morris.

"If you can fill the unforgiving minute with sixty seconds' worth of distance run." How many times do we sit and pout about someone who's done us wrong, and just be so resentful of them and so angry? But what if we could replace those sixty seconds with sixty seconds of something positive?

"If you can talk with crowds and keep your virtue, Or walk with kings—nor lose the common touch."

My mother, who lived through tough economic times, and learned the lesson of sharing her blessings, always emphasized this line the most. She said we must always strive to be humble, especially when we possess great influence or power over others. Everyone from the most to the least fortunate deserves respect. And just as important, we should be our best selves no matter whom we're with, with no regard for their position or lack of one.

Life reinforced this lesson for me in many ways, from the tragic, to the humorous, to the compassionate.

When I was twelve, I remember my mother crying the night that Dr. Martin Luther King was shot in Memphis. My parents had gone to Memphis that day to get my aunt Marilyn and uncle Bill from the airport. Their visit had been planned for months. The horrible crime had caused traffic jams and roadblocks, and what should have been a two-hour trip home turned into a five-hour drive.

My brothers and I had heard the news about the assassination on TV, and once my parents arrived home we could tell that there had been some very serious talk in the car about what had happened.

The whole family grieved, not only for Dr. King, but for the many black friends we had in Amory who were so traumatically affected by his death. We knew that his assassination was prompted by a hatred among a segment of the population who were not brought up to be comfortable around people different from themselves. In my house we knew that we were all members of the human race, no matter what our skin color.

———

A few years ago, I stopped for gas in Meridian, Mississippi. As I stood at the gas pump in my suit, a lady walked up and asked, "Has anyone ever told you that you look like Sam Haskell?" When I'm in Mississippi, I'm often asked if I AM Sam Haskell, but I'd never been told that I *looked* like Sam Haskell. I calmly replied, "You know, I get that all the time, but to be perfectly honest, Sam is a lot thinner than I am. But thanks for the compliment!"

Sometimes you are a king, and sometimes you are just a common man. It helps to be comfortable being either!

———

A girl in my high school class (let's call her Janice) came from a family without means. Her hair was often unkempt and her clothes old. She'd been held back more than once in school. Her father distributed the Tupelo *Daily Journal,* and Janice and her little sister would go out every morning at four o'clock to throw papers with their father. Their family was always on my mother's Christmas list when she and I drove around Amory delivering all of her presents on Christmas Eve. We usually had to walk over a newspaper-covered front porch to ring the bell and wait for Janice or her sister to answer the door.

If anyone represented the common man, they did.

But some of the kids in the high school treated her as less than common. In the cafeteria at lunch, Janice always sat by herself while the other kids shot spitballs at her table and teased her. She touched my heart and I thought she deserved better, but I had never done anything to stand up for her. Yes, I always spoke to Janice in the hall between classes, or if I ever saw her on the street in Amory. But doing it in front of my friends was different—until the day in my senior year that I decided enough was enough and I sat with her at lunch. Of course, my buddies said, "Haskell, what's wrong with you?! You gonna take her to the prom?" But I hated seeing her sit alone and I was finally brave enough to do something about it.

Janice and I had a nice conversation about her classes—which ones she thought were hardest and which were her favorites. She loved home economics, as she liked to cook and sew. I talked about how hard calculus and trig were with Mr. Newman. She burst out laughing when I told her about the time Mr. Newman walked into class with a new pair of shoes, leaned against the radiator, and slipped and fell flat on his butt. She asked me about going to Ole Miss, and said she thought I would be a great doctor. She also asked about my mother, who was the school nurse. Like every other student, Janice had been to see her several times when she had been sick.

That was the only time we had lunch together, but at the end of the school year I gave her a big hug.

When I was in Amory many years ago, I ran into her sister, Ann, and heard that Janice had moved away. "Janice talked about you all the time," she told me. "She would say, 'Sammy Haskell is my friend.' You'll never know how much it meant to her that you had lunch with her that day."

I was amazed, and humbled, and glad I had instinctively acted the way I did. It's so important—in high school and beyond—to not segregate yourself in a clique, to not deny yourself the experience of "walking" with any kind of person. If you do, you'll also exclude yourself from learning about other aspects of life and other people. We don't have time for everything or everyone, but diversity of experience is life-enhancing. I am comfortable with almost everyone: from the Prince of England to the William Morris parking attendant; with Janice as well as with the former President and First Lady. If you accept others for who they are, they're more likely to accept you for who you are. In Hollywood, I was a king, of sorts, and I still treated everyone with equal respect. When, through my friendship with His Royal Highness the Prince Edward, I found myself among real royalty—as a *nobody*—I was delighted to discover that they treated me the way I hoped I had treated others: with grace and respect.

———

As an agent I accumulated a lot of power. Some of it came from working hard, some from my personal values, and some from the relationships I fostered and the clients I represented.

I didn't start out as powerful, but I always followed the same guidelines, no matter how much clout I had. I treated everyone the same. This wasn't routine practice in Hollywood, so you can imagine—especially when I was just starting out—how wonderful it was for me to work with people who shared my philosophy.

Lily Tomlin and her writing collaborator and partner Jane Wagner had won the Emmy for Outstanding Variety Special for Lily's CBS special *Lily: Sold Out,* with guest stars Jane Fonda and Dolly Parton. When she agreed to do another special for NBC, *Lily for President,* my boss, Deborah Miller, assigned me to be the packaging agent.

I knew I'd be under a great deal of pressure, but I knew that if I pleased Lily and Jane, it would serve me well. I was (and am) a huge Lily Tomlin fan, and from the first production meeting I felt a connection. Lily and Jane treated their staff, the other talent, and even their agent like they were the most important people in the world. Imagine that! In their eyes, we were all working for the same cause, contributing something for the greater good.

When a deal needed to be made for a costume designer, art director, choreographer, director, producer, or actor, Lily and Jane asked me to do it—and her senior agents at the office allowed me, the new kid on the block, to have the access.

Lily for President had a wild assortment of guest stars, including Jerry Mathers from *Leave It to Beaver,* and Regis Philbin, who was starring in an NBC daytime show with cohost Mary Hart. There was even a cameo performance from a former Miss Mississippi who was near and dear to my heart: my fiancée, Mary Donnelly.

On the last day of filming, a couple of extras booked to play Richard Nixon and Fidel Castro did not show up. Lily, Jane, and the producer came to me in the production office, where I was helping the production secretaries type deal memos.

Lily and Jane said, "We have two questions: How far do you live from NBC, and do you have a navy pin-striped suit?"

I lived fifteen minutes away, and I had the suit. Lily told me to get it quickly. "I want you to play Richard Nixon, wearing a rubber Nixon Halloween mask." The skit involved Nixon and Castro and Tomlin's character Ernestine, outside President Tomlin's office at the White House.

I didn't blink, went straight to my apartment, and within an hour I was on set playing Richard Nixon.

Why did they ask me? I think it's because I was a polite, hardworking guy who helped them in every way I could. And because I was in the right place at the right time. And because they were inclusive and didn't think the favor was either beneath me or over my head. I wasn't the kind of agent they were used to. Most agents would have dropped by the set, said hello, and left. Before they met me, Lily and Jane didn't even know that there was more to be had. But they had inspired me, so I stuck around.

I confess: I so loved what I was doing that I took every opportunity to embrace it and really breathe it all in. For so long, I had wanted to be a part of this world. Now that I was in it, I grabbed every chance to learn—but I acted the same way whether I was with a superstar or a network page.

After the taping, Lily sent me a gift: an autographed photo of Ernestine with Richard Nixon and Fidel Castro, signed, "To Sam: Thanks for helping us save the world."

In the years that followed, no matter what my title at the office, I often became a confidant to my producers and my actors, and they asked me to be involved in most every decision.

I believe that during my time at William Morris, I changed many people's perception of agents. I wanted clients to know we cared about and believed in them. That was a new recipe for success that no one had really tried before—and it was all based on being able to walk with kings or the common man and treat everyone the same, myself included.

Later, I would pass along that ethic to the agents who worked for me. "We're going to do this together, shoulder to shoulder, as a team. My friend Greg Lipstone shared the following: Together Everyone Achieves More: T-E-A-M. Let's embrace each other and make this the best that it can be."

⸻

My mother discovered my obsession with English royal history when I was in the third grade. She'd found me reading a grown-up book on Queen Elizabeth I—*Good Queen Bess*—that I'd brought home from the school library. Then she confided that she, too, loved the royal family. It was one of our shared secrets.

Each book sent me to another book, and another book, and I became obsessed with the story of Henry VII and the War of the Roses and the defeat of Richard III in 1485. Then I started reading about Henry VIII and his six wives. That led me to Mary,

Queen of Scots and Lady Jane Grey. Then the Stuarts uniting England and Scotland.

I was so passionate about the subject that when I was thirteen, I decided to write to Queen Elizabeth II. I wanted to make sure the letter was exactly right, so my mother found some information about royal etiquette that explained how to properly address a monarch. The letter was three pages long and handwritten. In it, I told the Queen all that I knew about the history of her family, and about all the kings and queens of England. I also told her that I thought she was beautiful and that, since she had children close to my age, I'd absolutely love to travel to Great Britain to meet her and her family. I asked my father, "If the Queen says I can come to London to meet her, you'll fly me there, right?" "Oh, sure," my father said.

Then I included my Boy Scout picture, addressed the letter to Buckingham Palace, and dropped it into the mailbox.

Several months later, I was working at the Amory Public Library, shelving books, when my mother rushed in, saying, "Sammy, Sammy, where's Sammy?" in a loud whisper. She was wide-eyed when she found me. "You have a letter," she said, catching her breath, "from Balmoral Castle in Scotland!" Jean Jesse, the assistant librarian, joined us and we all read it together. The Queen's lady-in-waiting, Kathryn Drysdale, had written to me personally.

Balmoral Castle: Dear Samuel, I am commanded by Her Majesty the Queen to thank you for your recent letter of February 13, 1969, wherein you state that you would like to meet Her Majesty. Although Her Majesty wishes it were possible to meet the many visitors who travel to the United Kingdom each and every year, she can only give an audience to those recommended by the Ambassador to the Court of St. James. Her Majesty was most interested in seeing the photograph of yourself that you in-

cluded in your letter, and I have returned it herein as Her Majesty thought your mother would like to have it back. I remain, Sincerely Yours, Kathryn Drysdale, Lady-in-Waiting to Her Majesty the Queen Elizabeth II.

Of course, no one from Amory, Mississippi, would ever be able to get in touch with the American ambassador to the Court of St. James and get him to mention to the Queen, perhaps during a Buckingham Palace garden party, that she needed to meet me. I satisfied myself with having the letter framed and hung in the living room of our home so that anyone who ever came to our house knew that I had gotten a letter from Her Majesty the Queen!

I'd walked with other "kings" in my young life—my coach, my pastor, my scoutmaster—but I've never forgotten being treated so kindly by real royalty.

In fact, I've only written three fan letters in my entire life. The other two were to Lucille Ball and Judy Garland. They didn't answer, but I ended up representing their children, Lucie Arnaz and Liza Minnelli, as well as Queen Elizabeth's son, Prince Edward.

––––––

Although Mary and I had met Her Majesty Queen Elizabeth II at Edward and Sophie's wedding on June 19, 1999, at Windsor Castle, it wasn't until 2006—when His Royal Highness the Prince Edward and his brother, His Royal Highness the Prince Andrew, were inducted by Her Majesty The Queen into The Most Noble Order of the Garter—that we were blessed to spend a great deal of time with Her Majesty, the day before the ceremony.

First, Prince Edward, Mary, and I attended church (matins) with Her Majesty the Queen; His Royal Highness the Prince Philip; Edward and his brother, Prince Andrew; and Andrew's daughters Princess Beatrice and Princess Eugenie, at the Chapel at Royal Lodge, followed by cocktails with the family at Royal Lodge itself, located in Windsor Great Park.

Then we went to Frogmore, another Royal Residence in Windsor Great Park. After Princess Sophie had served a picnic lunch at Queen Victoria's Tea House, Prince Edward took Mary and me on a walking tour of Frogmore, including the Royal Burial Ground. The house dates back to the 1680s and the reign of King Charles II and was briefly the home of Queen Victoria's mother, The Duchess of Kent. Frogmore, which gets its name from the abundance of frogs living in this low-lying and marshy area, is very close to Windsor Castle and is also the site of the Royal Mausoleum containing the tombs of Queen Victoria and Prince Albert. As we were completing our tour of the Burial Ground, I said, "Oh Edward, can we *please* go inside the mausoleum?"

"I knew you were going to ask to do that," he said, somewhat sternly. "No one goes into Queen Victoria's mausoleum." He paused, and then, with a smile that meant he'd been teasing me, added, "Oh . . . let me go get the key."

Mary and I stood outside the mausoleum, waiting for Edward and a caretaker to return. Suddenly, we heard barking. A corgi came down the path, followed by a second and a third. "Oh my," Mary gasped. "I think The Queen is coming." I ran down the mausoleum steps and, out walking her dogs in her own garden, we came face-to-face with Her Majesty The Queen. Thank goodness we had met earlier that morning at church.

She walked right up to us. I told her we were waiting for Prince Edward and a key to the mausoleum, and we began to chat. It was the most wonderful conversation; she was so kind and charming. For the little boy who had admired the Queen forever, this was almost too exciting to bear. Of course, I remained calm, but afterward I was just so over the moon about it that I told everyone. My friends asked, "Did you tell her about the letter you sent her when you were a little boy? Did you?"

I suppose I could have said, "Your Majesty, let's sit on this bench so I can tell you a little story." But I didn't want to come across that way. I decided I'd rather just be an interesting person who knows a lot of English history, who respects the traditions and the monarchy, and who just happens to be a good friend of her son's. I know that's why Edward has always been keen on giving Mary and me access to his family's history and traditions—he knows we truly relish and appreciate it.

However, during a private tour of the Windsor Library at Windsor Castle, which is basically the Queen's private museum with artifacts from every monarch of England—there's an original Gutenberg Bible, racks of original Raphaels and da Vincis, the original death mask of Queen Elizabeth I—I innocently asked what's stored in the round tower of Windsor. It's the centerpiece of the castle. The docent's answer nearly knocked me off my feet. "Among other things, it's where all of the royal correspondence is kept. Every single letter that the Queen has received or answered is in that tower." I barely resisted the urge to barge in and search under H.

Several months ago, I realized I'd never told Edward about the letter to his mother. I don't know why, exactly, but it just never came up. When I finally shared the story with him, he was charmed hearing about my three fan letters and that I actually ended up representing each of their children. Knowing Edward, he may go to Windsor Castle one weekend in the very near future and, as a surprise, spend time looking through the Queen's correspondence under the letter H! If he does, I promise I'll act surprised.

Thanks to my mother's making me read Kipling's "If" and then showing me time and time again how the poem could be applied in life, I'll probably get the chance.

NINE

(Don't Be Afraid to) Stand in the Light

You intended to harm me, but God intended it for good to accomplish what is now being done, the saving of many lives.

—GENESIS 50:20

Nearly all men can stand adversity, but if you really want to test a man's character, give him power. —ABRAHAM LINCOLN

The year 1997 was an outstanding one for me. Everything good happened. Every deal closed. Lily Tomlin hosted a dinner at which I was honored by the Alliance for Children's Rights as their Man of the Year. The L.A. Mission honored me with their "Men Helping Women" award. I was the de-facto Worldwide Head of Television and on the fast track to becoming president of the William Morris Agency. My then-seven-year-old daughter, Mary Lane, was chosen to be on the pilot of Bill Cosby's version of the show *Kids Say the Darndest Things* for CBS.

In June, the week of my forty-second birthday, *People* magazine ran a big article about the kids we'd helped go to college through the Mary Kirkpatrick Haskell Scholarship Foundation and our biannual "Stars Over Mississippi" concerts. The *People* writer, who had followed me around for two months, at one point asked me to name the most important thing that had happened to me in Hollywood. Of what was I the most proud? I'm sure she expected to hear about Bill Cosby's latest deal, or something I helped make happen for George Clooney, Debbie Allen, or Kathie Lee Gifford.

"I guess what I'm most proud of," I said, thinking of how I'd determined to be one person for everyone so I could be comfortable anywhere and avoid personal artifice, "is that I'm exactly the same guy today that I was when I arrived here in 1978."

I think that surprised her. Sure, experience had made me savvier and more polished, but inside I felt exactly the same: I had the same values, same morals, same core. Even if I now bought my suits at Barneys instead of Belk, I was still essentially the same person as when I'd left Mississippi almost twenty years earlier.

The writer then asked for the names of some of my really important friends for comments. I gave her Leslie Moonves, president of CBS; Warren Littlefield, president of NBC; Phil Hartman, Bill Cosby, and George Clooney. Any of them would have given her a good quote. To my surprise, she talked to the parking attendant in the William Morris garage instead, who said, "Mr. Haskell always tells us 'Good morning' and 'Good night,' and he's one of the few who brings us something at Christmastime. He's always the same."

After I retired from William Morris in 2004, a secretary who was stationed on the path to my office when I walked in every morning, wrote and told me it meant a lot to her that I always greeted her as I passed her desk. To her, I was one of the most important men in the company. To me, she was just a human being like the rest of us, who deserved common courtesy. "Thank you," she wrote. "Your saying hello to me always made me feel good about myself."

Both of those comments, from people I saw on a daily basis, brought a smile to my face. They told me that I'd kept the promise I'd made to my mother about living my life "standing in the light." She never tolerated anything less from me. And, of course, my wife wouldn't have put up with less for a Mississippi minute.

———

It might sound strange for me to say that Hollywood and Mississippi are anything alike, but in truth most people in Hollywood are just regular workingmen and -women. Despite what you hear, it's not a terrible place filled with dishonest and cravenly ambitious people. There are a few powerful people who do things the wrong way, and that unfortunately creates a bad reputation for everyone. I have always been determined to be described differently. I wanted to be the honest, buttoned-down, character-driven guy who just so happened to be an agent.

I'll go even further. When I got to Hollywood, it's not that I discovered that agents didn't have good character; I just don't think character was ever discussed in the workplace. I knew plenty of agents who had character, it just wasn't cool to talk about it in a business where you have to make people believe you'd sell your children to make a great deal. Agents' marching orders were, "Go kill 'em and make the best deal you can." If handling people with integrity was part of it, let's just say it was never emphasized.

Through my motivational sessions at the company retreats I had figured out a way to insert good character into our daily work ethic. Some agents didn't like it, because it reminded them of what they weren't doing. But for the most part, especially among the younger ranks, who were still impressionable, they loved it because they realized that they didn't have to sell their souls to be successful. And if I detected a conflict, I wasn't afraid to mentor someone I felt was struggling. I made it my mission to listen to, teach, and empower my coworkers regardless of whether they worked in the mailroom or the boardroom.

———

Yes: 1997 was one of the best years of my life. And yet, as you'll now see, it was also one of the worst.

As my star began to shine—the story in *People,* for instance—some people I believed were my friends inexplicably began to pull back and act differently toward me. Suddenly, some of my agency friends didn't have time to go out to lunch. They didn't hang out in my office anymore. I would hear that so-and-so had said, "Sam doesn't deserve the attention." It seemed a strange reaction to my good fortune, and it made me really uncomfortable. Something had definitely changed.

To be fair, maybe some people were afraid all the attention *would* change me, so they became proactively defensive. Or was it jealousy? Resentment? I didn't know. Had I changed, maybe just a little? I was pretty sure it wasn't me; Mary would most definitely have told me if it was.

The cool treatment hurt. I didn't sleep well. Food didn't taste as good. I dreaded going to work in the mornings: me, the first one in, the last to leave. By show business standards, I had reached the top . . . and I was miserable. This wasn't right, and I knew it.

This bothered me so much that I went to see our pastor, Carolyn "Care" Crawford. I said, "Should I try to keep a lower profile? Should I not take credit for the work I do? Am I wrong to want to enjoy my successes? Why are some people acting this way?"

Believe me, I had worked for years in the shadows of others and I functioned quite well there, burying my ego, knowing my place as number two for my then-bosses Jerry Katzman and Bob Crestani. It pleased me to please them.

What my pastor heard from me was similar to situations she'd encountered with other parishioners: We can mourn and long for a life where we have to be less than we can be in order to make others comfortable. She let me know what she no doubt told everyone: "Your talents aren't yours to squander. They are a gift from God and you have a responsibility to use them, not hide them."

As guidance, she read a passage from Marianne Williamson's book *A Return to Love.*

> *Our deepest fear is not that we are inadequate. Our deepest fear is that we are powerful beyond measure. It is our light, not our darkness that most frightens us. We ask ourselves, Who am I to be brilliant, gorgeous, talented, fabulous?*
>
> *Actually, who are you* not *to be? You are a child of God. Your playing small doesn't serve the world. There is nothing enlightened about shrinking so that other people won't feel insecure around you. We are all meant to shine, as children do. We were born to manifest the glory of God that is within us.*
>
> *It's not just in some of us; it's in everyone. And as we let our own light shine, we unconsciously give other people permission to do the same. As we are liberated from our own fear, our presence automatically liberates others.*

Pastor Crawford said, "Perhaps you remind some people of what they are not, and they can't handle it. Don't change a single thing you're doing."

"That seems so prideful," I said. "I'm no better or worse than anyone else."

"Correct. And that's why you shouldn't change," she said. "You're not trying to make other people feel bad. Just be who you are."

Care helped me to see that I shouldn't feel guilty and diminish myself to give others a sense of comfort. When we stand in the light of God's grace and blessings, and we share those blessings, we're sharing the positive parts of ourselves. How can that be wrong?

I recently had a conversation with our daughter, Mary Lane, that reassured me that I'd somehow passed on the lesson of standing in the light to the next generation.

Mary Lane is very wise, but she wears her heart on her sleeve and wants to please everyone, just like her dad. She told me that during a college lecture, one of her NYU professors had said, "High visibility can be a trap and can make you more of a target."

Mary Lane said, "I stood up and told him, 'Visibility *can* make you a target *unless* you have the character to make your visibility truthful, faithful, and genuine. Then there is nothing to attack.'"

That floored me. My eighteen-year-old daughter already knew what it had taken me years to learn: We must not let the negative feelings of *others* distract us from standing in the light. As long as we're not *trying* to make them feel inadequate, we should not hide our talents.

———

Even though this is not a Hollywood memoir, I've never talked publicly before about leaving William Morris. Some of the people who read this will be happy, some won't. But that doesn't matter to me; it's my story, I lived it, and I'll tell it truthfully and in my own way because once again the experience contained a big lesson for me. This is the story of that lesson and of the struggle I went through to keep my promise to my mother to always stand in the light.

To understand this part of my life, it's helpful to understand the structure of the William Morris Agency. We had a chairman of the board, a chief executive officer, a president, a chief operating officer, a chief financial officer, a Worldwide Head of Television, a Worldwide Head of Music, and a Worldwide Head of Motion Pictures. This group made up the Executive Committee of the agency, and each of us served on the William Morris board of directors. With the exception of the chairman, the president, and the CEO, the other five of us were executive vice presidents. Serving under us were dozens of vice presidents and agents working in every department in the company. Each of the executive vice presidents had at least fifty people reporting to us, and we reported to the CEO. The television department had historically made the most money for the company, but the motion picture division provided the prestige. We had television hits like *The Cosby Show, Everybody Loves Raymond, The Fresh Prince of Bel-Air, Murphy Brown, Lost,* and *Who Wants to Be a Millionaire,* and our motion picture stars included Russell Crowe, Eddie Murphy, Catherine Zeta-Jones, James McAvoy, and Michael Douglas.

In 1999, I had been poised to become the next president of William Morris; I had been promised the position by my partners on the Executive Committee. It was a big deal, because TV agents rarely held that job. No one denied that I had earned it, but suddenly several members of the Executive Committee decided that we needed to poach a fierce competitor with big clients to shore up our flagging movie division.

Jim Wiatt was the cochairman of a rival agency, ICM. But he would only join us if we named him president of the company.

Needless to say I was disappointed, but my partners promised that he'd hold the title for two years, max, then move up. I would then be made president. This scenario was fine with me, as the title didn't mean as much to me as the opportunity that came with it to influence the character and direction of the company. I've never been a slave to titles. Once before, I had been asked to defer a promotion "for the good of the company," and being a team player, I did. And for the most part, it had worked out fine.

However, this time I had a bad feeling that we hadn't hired a team player. I had now been at the company for over twenty years. Walter Zifkin, the man who had hired me, knew I was wary, and he asked me to trust him.

Zifkin wanted a unanimous vote from the Executive Committee to show the entire company that this was a group decision. He also wanted my solemn promise that I would become Jim's friend and help him in every way I could. "Jim will need you," he said. I promised, hoping we were doing the best thing for the company and that we'd all be happy in the end.

I also agreed because I was committed to being a peacemaker. My mother first told me that I was a peacemaker when I was ten years old, because she had noticed how I'd settled a problem between a couple of school friends. She took it as a sign of my character.

"God puts certain people on this earth to calm the storms of life, to bring peace to disturbing or hurtful situations," she explained. "But being a peacemaker comes with great responsibility and reward." Then she quoted a verse from Jesus' Sermon on the Mount, "Blessed are the peacemakers, for they shall be called the children of God."

"You are a child of God," she said, "and I am very proud of the young man you are."

I realized that my mother was also a peacemaker and could

never let anyone stay angry at someone else for too long. I was touched and humbled, and took my mother's faith in me to heart. I wanted to continue to make her proud of me. Looking back, I feel that she revealed part of my destiny to me that day, and I still remember the promise I made to her to search for peace in every situation that commanded it.

For the first six months I made it a point to be our new president's friend and confidant. I would never say anything negative about him or listen to negativity from others. It was hard because not everyone was happy, and my office had become a place everyone came to complain. Morale was in the toilet and the office was steeped in drama. But I thought I had things under control.

One day, Steve Kram, one of my best friends at the company, confronted me about my "Wiatt cheerleading."

"Why are you supporting this guy? Don't you know what he is saying behind your back?"

I hated to ask. "What?"

"Sam Haskell is a Clydesdale horse, trudging along with blinders on, supporting mediocrity, carrying everybody on his back."

Really? That was a bit hard to take. The success of the TV department was, for all practical purposes, the success of the agency. If I was carrying anyone on my back, Wiatt's motion picture department was included. But we weren't talking dollars or sense. I began to realize that we had completely different value systems, and values have always been more important to me than dollars. I was confused and angry. What he called "trudging" I thought of as hard work. "Supporting mediocrity" seemed just another way for an elitist to say that television was beneath them. Sometimes, I thought my motion picture partners would have preferred the ego boost of a hit feature package over the steady income stream of a successful series. But you need both! "Carry-

ing everybody on his back"? Well, I wasn't in the habit of drop-
ping people—agents or clients—when the chips were down, especially when they'd proven themselves by making money for the
company. And wearing "blinders" in Hollywood isn't necessarily
a bad thing; without them, you might lose sight of what's really
important—like your work, your word, loyalty, friendship, and respect. Wiatt was a quick study, and as soon as he discovered that
I was sensitive, he began to push those buttons to my face on a
regular basis. And behind my back.

Clearly, Wiatt and I were from different planets. When I discovered that he had undermined me not only with people in the
company, but with those outside, I felt sickened. How could this
happen?

I realized in that moment that in order to be a team player I
had become willfully blind and ignored the truth. I'd tried to be
positive and make the situation work, but now I felt as if my
world had been turned upside down. But I needed to keep walking straight, to focus on the principles I lived by, to stay in the
light.

Inside the agency, the focus began to shift. Where I had once
focused only on my clients, office politics had now invaded my
world. My days, never boring, had once run the emotional gamut
from total elation to total frustration; but now I began to feel as
if I were careening through a minefield.

Though I never let Wiatt know that I knew about what he was
saying behind my back, I got smarter in how I handled him. He
would tell my agents: "Your client list is not good enough, your
appearance is not suitable, you report to me, not to Sam," etc.
He constantly pushed the Executive Committee and tried to
take control of the television department, but I wouldn't give it
up. We had a strict hands-off policy. And besides, why fix what's
not broken? But his criticism of me and my staff continued.

"Sam should have a more impressive client list," he would tell people. "He should have Dick Wolf (*Law & Order*) as a client. Why can't he sign Steven Bochco (*Hill Street Blues*)?"

He went further: "Sam spends too much time trying to nurture his agents and clients. He's too nice."

I listened to each suggestion (criticism?) he offered. If it made the least bit of sense to me, I would try to address it; otherwise, I dismissed it. But I would not and could not give him control. Nor did I feel I ever had to defend myself or my client list. My success at the William Morris Agency spoke for itself.

Then, to my complete surprise, several William Morris agents were fired when I was out of town. To me, this represented a complete violation of our usual hands-off policy—the decision should never have been made, let alone implemented, behind my back. We did have to let some people go, but these agents were designated to undergo further review. I thought at least three were productive and with some redirection could continue to be very influential and profitable members of our company. I wanted to reconsider and perhaps save some of their jobs, but I was in Williamsburg, Virginia, chaperoning Sam IV's sixth-grade class, having a difficult time with the school's headmaster.

If God has a sense of humor, on this journey it wasn't part of the plan.

Like some of my partners at William Morris, the school headmaster could be very uptight, to say the least. He had rules that few of us could understand. I kept wondering, What are the lessons for me here?

One of the kids was very bright, yet troubled. He sometimes vomited or had accidents just because he was insecure about being away from his parents. Every time something went wrong, the headmaster said, "Mr. Haskell, clean it up." I did.

Then one of the mothers—the only one who'd been on the

trip twice—took me aside. She said, "I've got good news and bad news for you."

"Okay."

"The good news is, you're the most important parent on this trip."

"What's the bad news?"

"The bad news is, you're going to be cleaning up vomit and s**t the rest of the trip. The headmaster picks on who he perceives to be the most powerful or influential parent and makes them do the most menial chores."

I figured I could handle that, even if I didn't like it.

Later that night, a couple of kids in my group got into a fight with another chaperone's son. One of the boys' mothers had come into the room to help settle it. We weren't allowed to associate with our own kids on the trip, for fear of making the other children jealous—another one of the headmaster's crazy rules. When the headmaster and I walked in, the boys were all in their boxers, getting ready for bed. He ordered the mother out. She tried to explain, but he insisted. When she left, she flipped him off behind his back. All the boys laughed, and even I had a little trouble stifling a chuckle.

Of course, he became furious at the laughter—though he didn't know the reason for it. He escorted the four roommates out onto the balcony.

This was the last straw. "This is wrong," I said. "I'm not going to allow you to do this. These boys could get sick. And even if they don't, it's wrong. I don't care what you think of me, but they are not standing out here. If you want to have a conversation with them about fighting or who stole whose money, we're going to do it inside, and they're going to be allowed to put their clothes on. Boys, come inside."

The headmaster went away, red-faced and fuming.

I took the boys back into the room and they put their pajamas on. I told them that the headmaster would return in a minute. He never came back, and he didn't mention the incident again.

That evening I checked in with my office. A fellow father, my roommate and friend Steve Albright, watched my face as my assistant filled me in about the firings. I had a meltdown. From Williamsburg, I called every agent who'd been fired to tell them I would miss them and to thank them for their years of service to the agency. Each of them found jobs immediately, and today many of them are quite successful.

But it meant I'd also be cleaning up some vomit and s**t when I got back to the office.

———

I flew back to Los Angeles realizing that in order to stand in the light and not feel miserable, I needed to take as strong a stand within the company as I had with the headmaster. But I'd done it before and knew I could do it again.

I recalled an incident that motivated me to stand up for what I thought was right. During a weekly management meeting, I had given my TV department financial report. Our numbers were multiples higher than the motion picture numbers. Irritated, someone said, "You know, William Morris's motion picture department is like a fine Mercedes dealership—sleek cars with perfect detail and accessories—and the television department is like a Chevrolet dealership—one plain car after another pushed out on a conveyor belt, with nothing unique or classy about it." I bit my tongue to see if anyone else would speak up. No one did. Finally, I calmly replied, "You know, while people are only browsing in the Mercedes dealership, they're buying the frigging Chevrolets, and that's what keeps the lights on around here!"

The next several years were excruciating. Wiatt did not move up the corporate ladder and allow the board's promise to me to be fulfilled. But I could not give up. I had promised my mother to never let the dark side prevail. I loved William Morris and I loved almost everyone who was a part of it. I told myself that it just had to get better. But it didn't.

By the beginning of 2004, the atmosphere at the office had deteriorated so much that I had to stop at my church on the way to work to pray for the strength to get through each day—especially Thursdays, when we had management meetings. Battles were constant; issues of titles and control were prevalent; and the random hiring and firing of employees was getting worse. I went to bed every night with a headache and woke up every morning with a stomachache. My presidency of the company was delayed over and over again.

Then I suddenly remembered something my father had said when I started at William Morris. "Play in the toy shop, but don't become one of the toys." He meant that if you become one of the toys, then you're not the one playing, you're being played *with*.

I had reached a point where I felt that the culture I had helped build at William Morris couldn't be preserved and maintained, and ultimately run the way I thought best. How could I stay and allow a management shift in philosophy, when I knew in my heart of hearts that I didn't believe in it, and knew that it wouldn't work in the long run?

Just as I had watched the cancer that had moved through my mother's body destroy her strength, her confidence, and her resolve, I now witnessed the slow but deliberate destruction of a world that meant so much not only to me, but to hundreds of my associates.

When summer arrived, I switched to a different prayer at church. Instead of asking for strength to get through the day, I asked God if this was what HE wanted for my life.

I hung in while I waited for God's answer. In September 2004, I agreed to become vice chairman of William Morris, and one of our motion picture partners would be named president. Then I left town to stage another "Stars Over Mississippi" concert in Amory. It was my biggest show ever and the pressure was intense, but I couldn't focus on it properly because of problems brewing in California. In my absence I discovered that several junior William Morris board members had started a discussion about removing a senior board member who was close to me. I should have expected it; something awful seemed to happen almost every time I left Los Angeles.

After I returned, and the insurrection had been squashed, a huge argument erupted in our Thursday management meeting. We were discussing whether or not to hire a new agent for a huge salary, even though he had only one profitable client. The management committee was split. After we explained that hiring this agent did not fit our business model, several members of the "opposition" got quite upset. Then one of them threw his luncheon plate of pasta against the boardroom wall. Everyone froze. I quietly picked up my plate of food, and asked, "Would you like to throw my plate, too?"

I'd hoped my comment would inject a little humor into the foul mood of the room, but it didn't work. He exploded and started banging his hands on the table, saying, "I have to have complete control, I have to have complete control."

To have any hope of winning this battle of values and culture, I realized, I'd have to cross a line—one I knew I couldn't, because I kept hearing my mother's voice in my head: "Stand in the light."

After many sleepless nights, the time had come to decide. It was them or me. I chose me. The decision was God's answer to my earlier prayers. I saw both forks in the road clearly and chose the one that took me into the light. I could be at William Morris right now, making loads of money, fighting the good fight, but it was no longer a war I wanted or felt I had to win, because winning meant losing what was most important to me: my self-respect.

———

On December 16, 2004, the entertainment trades reported that Worldwide Head of Television Sam Haskell, Chief Operating Officer Steve Kram, and Worldwide Head of Music Richard Rosenberg had left William Morris because of "philosophical differences as to how the company should be run." Some executives inside and outside the agency would say that our departure signaled a fundamental change in the agency's DNA. Those who knew me best knew that even in their simplest form, my reasons for leaving were complicated.

The encouragement and support that flowed my way, however, was *not* complicated. Afterward, I received over fourteen hundred calls, e-mails, and personal letters—and I answered every one of them. My friends called with job offers at cable networks and studios. Nancy Josephson, of the Endeavor Agency, called two or three times a week with ideas *and* offers. The reaction to my departure fell into four categories: 1.) Those who thought my leaving was great and encouraged me to "go change the world." 2.) Those who asked, "What about me?" meaning clients and fellow agents who would miss my professional presence in their lives. 3.) Those who asked, "Are you going straight to Washington?"—as if I would become Jimmy Stewart in *Mr. Smith Goes to Washington*. Some people even sent checks made out to "The Committee to Elect Sam Haskell." I returned each one with a personal note of thanks, and the promise to contact them again one day if I ever decided to pursue a political career. 4.) Those who thought I had been fired.

Yes, fired. When a school bully confronted my daughter, Mary Lane, during a lunch break and said, "My dad told me that your father was fired and that he's not a big shot anymore," Mary Lane's very calm response was "Tell your father that MY father is too important to be fired." This didn't happen on a primary school playground, but in high school. I was surprised at the cruelty of that boy *and* his father, but I explained to Mary Lane that while I was not fired, in life, *no one* is ever too important to be fired. Unfortunately, it happens every day.

I was not at all angry at the William Morris Agency. I'd made the decision to leave. And I didn't want to say bad things about a company that had given me such a wonderful opportunity to do terrific things for myself, my family, and others. Plus some good friends were still there.

When the press called, I refused all interviews. The details of the infighting would have fed the show business gossip machine for a week, then been forgotten. I never really wanted to explain anything unless the day came that a lesson might be shared through the story of an ordinary man placed in extraordinary circumstances—and how he handled himself.

Mary showed me a card once that read, "We plan and God watches. . . . We pray and God answers." That says it all, doesn't it? This is where faith and understanding come in. This is where all the principles I try to live by come to bear. I regret that my final years at William Morris were so difficult, but I now see those years as divine intervention. Leaving allowed me to take the next steps in my life, instead of continuing to run in place.

———

When we come to a crossroads, character must take over. We sometimes say, "Where there's a will, there's a way." To most people this phrase means that if there's a way to power through something, or if we personally have the will to make something happen, we should try to do so. I see this as seeking *God's* will for our lives so he can show us the way. Ironically, the most important thing I learned from my twenty-six years at William Morris wasn't how to put together number one shows. It was that God is in charge—not me.

Too many people in all walks of life compromise themselves because they fear that they don't have the strength to stand up and say no. I wanted to stand in the light, and nowhere else. Luckily, I'd worked hard to earn a good reputation, and it withstood the unhappy circumstances that led to my leaving.

In some ways, the situation at William Morris was as much a disappointment to me as not winning the Good Citizenship Award had been in middle school. Well, almost. Sometimes you work as hard as you can, and do everything to the best of your abilities, and life still doesn't turn out the way you expected it would. Just as in middle school, where I learned that doing everything right did not guarantee success, I began to realize that though the stakes at William Morris were a million times higher, the results and the lessons I could utilize to maneuver my way through *were exactly the same*. At least this time I hadn't banged on the piano keys (or the tabletop) to show my frustration and displeasure. So what looked to some like losing wasn't losing at all. And I didn't have to seek out a new version of my teacher Mike Justice to tell me where I'd gone wrong.

———

The day before my resignation was announced, I had an unexpected visitor in my office—and I mean *really* unexpected! He had come to ask for my forgiveness for how he had treated me and for how events had turned out and—I couldn't believe I was hearing this—he had also come to ask me to stay. "I've got to know that you can forgive me," he said. "You're a Christian; that's what you're supposed to do."

Amazing. I couldn't stay, but I did hug and forgive him. And, as I looked back on the five and a half years of daily battles, protecting my people, and all the rest, it struck me that perhaps this surprise visit was not motivated by guilt or remorse—perhaps he simply had his way of doing business and I had mine, and the twain just couldn't meet. Perhaps his last-minute visit was simply his natural human instinct to want to be remembered as standing in the light. I hope so.

Make Stone Soup

There's a classic children's story called "Stone Soup." There
are many versions. The one I remember best described
three hungry soldiers going home after the Revolutionary War.
They come to a town, hoping to find something to eat. But the
townspeople don't know if these are good soldiers or bad soldiers,
so they remain huddled in their houses, afraid, and hide their
food—which is, as you can imagine, in short supply after years of
fighting.

The soldiers ignore the townspeople. Instead, they find an old black kettle, fill it with water, build a fire, and put the kettle on to boil. When the water bubbles, one soldier tosses a rock into the pot.

A moment later a woman comes out of her house and says, "What are you doing? Why did you put that rock in the water?"

"Making stone soup," says the soldier. He stirs the water, then puts in another rock. "It's very delicious."

Soon someone else asks the same question. "Making stone soup," the soldier says.

"I have a piece of beef put away," said one woman. "I have some corn," said another.

Slowly, one by one, the townspeople venture into the square, and each puts something into the pot. One has a handful of rice, another some spices, a third carrots, others chicken and beans. Before long the kettle is filled with the most wonderful stew.

The soldiers had done this before, and knew that by contributing what they had—and they had nothing, so they had to make do with stones—the townspeople might become curious and venture out and contribute as well. The result: The whole town, and the soldiers, would be able to eat because they'd overcome their suspicions and shared.

To understand the message of *Stone Soup* is to understand the importance of philanthropy. Mary and I have been making friends and "stone soup" since we began dating in 1976. Whatever else we've done, giving back has always been part of our lives, and in so doing we continue to honor the promise I made to my mother to remember that a blessing is not a blessing unless it is shared. If we all give the best we have, we can stir up a soup that will nourish the world.

When we share we shine.

In the Cub Scouts, we'd make arts and crafts, take them to the old folks' home, and hand them out as Christmas gifts. In the Boy Scouts we did community service. Sometimes we'd hold money drives for different charities. We'd put up tripods with hanging buckets, almost like the Salvation Army, at Amory's main intersections, and stand around in our Scout uniforms, asking people to give us their change as they drove by.

Since drivers couldn't reach the buckets, we were supposed to go up to car windows, but I was so embarrassed I couldn't do it. It seemed like public begging. I was also sure no one would stop for me and I'd be humiliated.

"Why is this the only way that we can give back?" I whined to my mother. "Why is this how we're supposed to do it?"

My mother had to make certain I didn't let excuses stand in the way of an opportunity to share my blessings. She told me in no uncertain terms that *this was how it was done.* "You have been so blessed in your life. You have everything that you need. There are so many who don't. It doesn't matter if this is uncomfortable for you. You get out there with your troop members and stand at that intersection."

"But what if no one stops for me?" I said.

"It's not about you," she said. Then, because she couldn't resist being reassuring: "But there are plenty of people in town who know who Sammy Haskell is. They'll stop for you."

My mother was right. My bucket—like those of the other boys—was filled and refilled. I was so excited that I volunteered every weekend.

———

In 1992, I started the Mary Kirkpatrick Haskell Scholarship Foundation. As you know, my initial dream was to raise $1 million over ten years, staging the "Stars Over Mississippi" concerts with big stars, primarily my clients.

Unfortunately, that first year I had a big problem. This time I wasn't uncomfortable asking for contributions; everyone loved my mother and I knew they would give whatever they could. But some people in Amory simply didn't believe I could pull it off, and they spread rumors that I wouldn't—no, couldn't—actually get the stars.

Well, if not the stars, then what?

"He's going to bring look-alikes and sound-alikes," I heard. Clearly some imaginations had been working overtime. This was small-town mentality at its finest.

I told my aunt Betty how troubled I was about some of the townspeople's attitudes. She said, "What you need to remember, darling, is that to you, Amory, Mississippi, is a thousand wonderful people. The rest don't matter. You just need to focus on the thousand who love you, and who you love. Then everything will be all right."

I wasn't so sure. With a week to go we'd sold only three thousand tickets—and ticket sales were the only way I could pay for the scholarships. I'd used the corporate money I'd received for expenses: to fly everyone in, pay for the musicians, the stage, the sound, the lights, etc. I was nervous. I knew I had to make some stone soup, but what in the world was it going to taste like?

When I landed at the Memphis airport a few days before the show, I was overcome with worry. I needed something to reenergize me and lift my mood.

When I opened the rental car door I saw a shiny penny on the seat.

A lucky penny. A sign from my mother. I immediately felt better.

That penny made me work even harder to get the word out about the concert and foundation, and to convince people they could trust me.

I appeared on every TV and radio show that would book me.

My committee chairmen tripled their efforts at my urging, and we sold enough tickets after all—almost seven thousand.

The night before the first "Stars Over Mississippi" show, we'd scheduled a big gala at the Amory River Birch Country Club. All the celebrities—not look-alikes or sound-alikes!—would be there: Kathie Lee Gifford; Christian vocalist Sandi Patty; Debbie Allen; former Miss America Mary Ann Mobley and her husband, actor Gary Collins; comedian Wil Shriner; *Little House on the Prairie*'s Dean Butler; Mississippi actor Gary Grubbs; Tupelo native Guy Hovis, who'd been a star of *The Lawrence Welk Show*; and Mary Haskell.

In the car with Mary on the way to the event, I asked her, "How can I ever thank these people from my hometown? How can I possibly let them know how much I appreciate them having the faith to share with me so that I could share with others; having the faith that I could really do this?"

People from all over north Mississippi—not just Amory—had paid lots of money to be at the gala, to mix and mingle, and to have their pictures taken with the performers. At that first gala, we had a reception for three hundred and raised fifty thousand dollars above what we cleared the next night at the concert.

Mary said, "Why don't you tell the Cheer Man story."

"That's a great idea," I said. It made sense. After the Cheer Man came when I was a kid, everybody in school talked about it for two weeks and then it was forgotten. Now I was no longer a little boy, but I still had the same faith. In a way, everyone at the gala who had helped make my dreams come true were Cheer Men and Women.

That night I told the story, then said, "You all had the blind faith to believe in me, the purity of faith found in a child." And I thanked them for it, because in truth they hadn't known for sure that I would do what I said I would. "Just as I believed the Cheer Man would come to Amory, Mississippi, you believed that Sam

Haskell would bring these stars to Amory, and raise this money, and give scholarships to kids in northern Mississippi to go to college."

As I spoke, I could see some childhood friends in the audience who had actually been in our front yard for my brother's ninth birthday. They were nodding their heads.

The next day, during our first parade down Main Street, people brought Cheer boxes, with brightly colored balloons attached, and held them high.

I have subsequently organized seven "Stars Over Mississippi" concerts in twelve years, and we have raised over $4 million to put about five hundred kids and counting through college in Mississippi. The money came from Amory, from all over Mississippi and the South, from California and New York. I had sponsorships from movie studios and television networks. My mentors at William Morris were always generous. My good friend Leslie Moonves gave me five thousand dollars every year for the foundation. Generous donations were also made by Gail Berman at Fox, Andrea Wong at ABC, Jeff Zucker at NBC, Peter Roth and Bruce Rosenblum at Warner Bros., and Steve Mosko at Sony. Jason Winters and Erik Sterling raised hundreds of thousands of dollars to support my cause. Wal-Mart, Viking Range, Northwest Airlines, and BancorpSouth became the primary patrons of the foundation. These special friends and many others all embraced and supported my dream.

Sometimes dreams really do come true.

Of course, that doesn't mean I accomplish everything I'm determined to accomplish. After I told the Cheer Man story someone came up and said, "What is this about winning ten dollars! Why didn't you wish for the Publishers Clearing House Sweepstakes?"

If I'd only known. Well, I guess there's still time for that!

In late August of 2005, Mary and I were in Madison, Mississippi. She had a concert at a Baptist church, and I had been invited to give the keynote address. But all anyone talked about the entire weekend was the hurricane heading toward the Gulf Coast.

When Hurricane Camille had struck Mississippi in 1969, no one thought there could ever be anything worse. The winds reached 190 miles per hour, a record at the time. Other hurricanes have since come and gone. The residents of Gulfport and Biloxi are accustomed to boarding up their windows and leaving for a couple of days, then coming back when the storms subside.

But this was different. That day I kept hearing, "This is a big one. This is a big one." We did our appearance at the church, and the next morning we had brunch with a few of our friends. Someone said the hurricane was supposed to hit that night and that people were scared, and evacuations were under way as far north as Jackson, Mississippi, which was where we were eating, and where we were supposed to fly from to get back to Los Angeles.

When we walked outside the restaurant in Jackson, we realized the streets were filled with people desperately preparing for the worst, along with countless evacuees from the Gulf Coast.

By the time Mary and I got to the airport, so many people were jamming the terminals that our flights were either delayed or canceled. Seats were at a premium, and often only one was available on a flight. I had to go via Atlanta to get back home. Mary had to go to Dallas. It was chaos.

Hurricane Katrina hit land that night, and the next day the news was full of the worst devastation I'd ever seen. New Orleans, a national treasure, got most of the attention because the levees broke. But the hurricane had actually hit Mississippi.

Forty-one of eighty-two counties were declared national disaster areas.

As I lay safe in my bed in Los Angeles, watching the destruction on TV, I knew I had to do something to help. At first Les Moonves got me involved with *Shelter from the Storm: A Concert*. Joel Gallen, who'd done *America: A Tribute to Heroes After 9/11*, produced it. I got Morgan Freeman, Sela Ward, Ray Romano, Jason Alexander, Debra Messing, and many of my friends and clients to do little pieces for the show. I think they raised $20 or $25 million for the Red Cross and other groups.

But I knew that Mississippi needed more help. If I threw my desire and energy into the kettle first, perhaps I could get my friends to help make stone soup for the hurricane victims.

First I called Mississippi governor Haley Barbour, who gave me his blessing. I then called Jeff Zucker at NBC and said, "I'm going to put together a three-hour telethon live from Ole Miss. Can you give me time on MSNBC?" Zucker had supported *Shelter from the Storm: A Concert*. He asked what I had planned. My plan consisted of names: "I'm going to get Morgan Freeman, Whoopi Goldberg, Faith Hill, Sela Ward, Marilu Henner, Ray Romano, Macy Gray, Brian McKnight, Doris Roberts, Debbie Allen, Delta Burke, Gerald McRaney, Lance Bass, Kathy Ireland, Jason Alexander, Jean Smart, Marilyn McCoo, Billy Davis, Jr., Jill Conner Browne (*The Sweet Potato Queens*), Pam Tillis, Samuel L. Jackson—"

He cut me off: "Done."

My friend Michael Seligman wanted to help. The day after he produced that year's Emmys, he brought the entire Emmy crew to Mississippi to help us produce the show. My friend Lanny Griffith, a former lobbying partner of Governor Barbour, began raising corporate money. Wal-Mart, Viking Range, and BancorpSouth, three of my sponsors for "Stars Over Mississippi," stepped up again to help us with this worthy cause. So did my former client and friend Barry Manilow, who made a generous donation through the Manilow Foundation. Lanny, originally from Corinth, Mississippi, came up with the show title, *Mississippi Rising*. Steve Mosko from Sony, and friends at FedEx and Mississippi Power, provided their corporate jets. Morgan Freeman hosted.

In the end, I got forty-four stars to come to Mississippi.

I brought in the Bitch Patrol—Dot, Ellen, Jean, and their whole team of volunteers from Amory. With the help of my college friends, my cousins, and other longtime friends from Amory and Oxford, the Bitch Patrol took over and coordinated the volunteers from churches, the downtown stores, the drivers, and private lodging.

We don't have a Four Seasons Hotel in Oxford, Mississippi; the celebrities who wanted hotel rooms would have had to stay at a Day's Inn equivalent. Better, I thought, to put them in gorgeous homes with a loving family and have a beautiful suite of rooms at their disposal, where they could have a much better experience and a true taste of the South. So, our celebrities stayed in private homes, with volunteer escorts assigned to each one. Volunteers handled wardrobes, script pages, and performance needs. The local churches made all the food.

Kathy Ireland sent massive amounts of furniture, lamps, and rugs from her worldwide designer collection so we could create a giant Green Room in the concourse area of the Coliseum. She later donated all the furniture to the victims on the coast. Senator Trent Lott put Kathy's name in the U.S. Congressional Record as "The benevolent benefactress of Mississippi."

L.A. attorney Steve Albright, my good friend, flew to Mississippi and made airport runs and drove celebrities around for a week. Some of my former assistants at William Morris called to offer help, and I had jobs for each of them. One, Jim Morey's son, Jason, who had been my trainee at William Morris for a couple of years, left his job and came to be my assistant. Jason Morey took complete control of my life that week, and I can honestly say I couldn't have done it without him.

Fellow Mississippian Sela Ward was an incredible help to me in booking talent and offering emotional support. Sela constantly reminded me to rest and helped me manage my stress. She knows me so well, and I adore her. My former clients Pam Long and Paul Miller wrote and directed the show. Whoopi Goldberg and First Lady Marsha Barbour went directly to the coast to help the victims, and Whoopi hosted several documentaries on the destruction that we used in the show. Everyone near and dear to me had agreed to help.

Just before the show, we were waiting for Faith Hill to join everyone for a group photo. I could tell that some of the celebrities were anxious. I left my position in the risers, went down in front of everybody, and said, "You're either an old friend or a new friend of mine. But because you're here, you will always be very special to me." I could see some eyes starting to glisten. I went on, "For the rest of your lives, you will remember this date in October 2005 when you stood in the light of God's grace and did something good to help the people of Mississippi."

In nineteen days, we had structured and put on a show at the University of Mississippi Coliseum in Oxford that normally would have taken six months to mount. We raised $15 million initially. Then the show aired in Europe for three hours. The ripple effect of *Mississippi Rising* ended up raising over $30 million. Lanny Griffith and I worked diligently with Governor Barbour and the Mississippi Hurricane Recovery Fund to raise the money to help people rebuild their businesses, their churches, their schools, their homes, and their lives. The Recovery Fund filled in when insurance companies fell short. This money did a lot of good. The whole experience was a great example not only of making stone soup from scratch, but of being able to let a lot of light shine.

Mary later said, "It's never just about one ingredient. It's about how all the elements can come together to make something greater than the whole." And she was absolutely right.

Live a Principled Life

On this day, keep a promise. On this day, forget an old grudge. On this day, examine your demands on others and reduce them. On this day, fight for a principle. —ON THIS DAY, ANONYMOUS

Trying to live a principled life can be difficult. None of us is perfect, and we live in challenging times. There seems to be trouble coming every day, from every direction. People want something or someone to hold on to, something to give them hope, to help them understand the world and each other. The answer to what that is is different for everyone; my answer has always been to share my blessings and to focus on maintaining my character, in the belief that this can somehow benefit those around me. To borrow a slogan first coined by Patrick Geddes in 1915, I can "think globally and act locally." My life has been filled with positive and negative moments, and I try to pay attention, because every experience has a purpose.

I believe that part of my purpose is to share those promises I made to my mother, and I hope that you can identify with and embrace those promises too. I have had incredible experiences and wonderful life lessons that add up to a patchwork quilt that's both comforted and guided me. I want to wrap that quilt around others—not only to tell them about my journey, but also to help them on their own journeys.

A principled life is the road I'll always choose. To me, that means being devoted to your faith, your mate, your family; to a career, to community service, and to making a difference. Living a life of fidelity, honesty, fairness, understanding, facilitating good and strong relationships, and maintaining who you are. Doing anything that basically upholds the principles of the Ten Commandments.

But sometimes I find myself asking if that is even possible in these challenging times. When I was thirteen, if I had a friend whose father had a *Playboy* magazine that we could sneak a peek at (at the articles, of course), it was unbelievably great. We even got to see a naked girl! When I think about what today's kids have at their fingertips on the Internet, I'm anxious. When Mary and I fix a plate and watch TV instead of sitting down to a family dinner, I feel like I'm missing something from my past. When I find myself holding a grudge against someone who seems to have gotten his values from Saturday morning cartoons, I cringe. I have so many questions and concerns, every single day.

I don't mind the questions. Answering them is what life is all about. If everything were perfect, we'd be bored. If I could reassemble myself, you can bet there'd be things I'd change. But I wouldn't cut out *everything* about myself that I don't like, because those traits are what motivate me to continue to seek understanding and to try to improve. They give me a reason to get out of bed in the morning.

Everyone's heard the expression, "Reach your potential." I hope I never reach my potential, because if I do then I have nowhere to go but down. I'd cease to evolve. But if I continue standing in the light, always reaching for something more, reaching for that potential, then I'll always be looking up. That way I can constantly strive to be better every day.

This reminds me of a great one-panel cartoon I once saw in a newspaper. A toddler stands in a mess of unrolled toilet paper. The caption reads, "Be patient. God's still working on me." Well, God's still working on me, too. Growing me, leading me, loving me.

———

I believe my mother would be happy if she could see my life today. She'd know I've kept my promises to her: to share my blessings, to have faith in myself, to embrace change, to be kind, to find something to believe in, to treat everyone the same, to be a strong and fair parent, to never stop dreaming, to be a good friend, to keep God at the center of my life, to forgive, to resist jealousy, to never forget my character and integrity, to live every day to the fullest, and to never forget how much she loved me.

And being my mother, she'd still remind me to share my "time, talent, and treasure" wisely; to not get overtired or overpressured. A couple of years before she died, she was in L.A. for a visit with Mary and me, and after seeing how active we were in so many things, she told Aunt Betty that "Sam really needs a good recliner. They don't have a recliner for him to relax in like he had in my house." She's right. We had twin recliners in the den of my childhood home, and that's where Momma and I would have our holiday conversations. (I still don't have a recliner!)

My mother would have worshipped my children. In her eyes, they would have been the most perfect and beautiful boy and girl ever born. She most likely would not have wanted us to discipline them. Instead, she'd have counseled us to be more patient with them, and to never mention a word about what might be perceived as a fault—only what's positive and perfect. She absolutely believed in disciplining children, but in her mind, her grandchildren wouldn't have needed it. My mother thought of those she truly loved the way Melanie Hamilton Wilkes thought of Scarlett O'Hara in *Gone with the Wind*. Melanie could not imagine an imperfection, a moment of dishonesty or disloyalty or anything but positive traits in those she loved, and my mother was exactly the same way. Sam IV and Mary Lane would have held my mother in the palm of their hands!

My mother also would have loved my clients and my friends. I've often imagined a scene around my mother's kitchen table in Amory with Ray, Doris, Kathie Lee, Jason, Les, Erik, Debbie, Edward, and Sophie eating a home-cooked meal of fried chicken, fried squash, fried okra, corn on the cob, mashed potatoes, and homemade corn bread. This was the very meal she always cooked for me and my best friends on my birthday each June 24, and I've often thought about her cooking that same meal for my new but older friends.

She would have discussed my joys and anguish at William Morris, and taken personally anything that hurt me. But she would also have seen the "big picture," and probably wondered why it took me so long to realize that God had another plan for my life.

———

Having recently passed the half-century mark, I realized, as we all must at that moment, that life's journey was both half over and just beginning. Middle age sets the stage for another chapter of our adventures on earth. I'm also reminded that my mother-in-law, Shirley Donnelly, told me to challenge myself with a crossword puzzle each and every morning because it will keep my mind sharp. It's sure worked for her, so I'm trying it.

Now when I wake up each morning I am even more aware of

how incredibly blessed we all are. Recently, while talking with my good friend Don DeMesquita and enjoying my favorite breakfast at Jerry's Deli, I found myself telling him that if God forbid I get hit by a truck when leaving the restaurant, to please tell my family and friends that while I know they will miss me, they shouldn't waste any time worrying about a life cut short, or a life not lived. Like George Bailey, I, too, have had a wonderful life. My journey has taken me from a small town in northeast Mississippi to the great cities of the world, to the White House, to Buckingham Palace, and back again.

I wrote this book to share my blessings. I want to make a difference. There's lots of second-guessing going on in the world, so if I can play a small part in shining a light on some positive food for the soul, I will be happy. I have so many questions about life. Everyone does. But I know in my heart that the answer to life's mysteries can't possibly all be revealed to us during our brief sojourns on earth.

If God chose to call me home today, I'd want everyone to know that my life here had been full of joy, adventure, love, loss, and laughter. I know that would make my Momma proud. I've kept my promises to her, and I know that hers will be the first face I see, hers will be the first hand I touch, and hers will be the first voice I hear, as she leads me to the one who will finally answer all of my questions.

Selected Poetry

THE GUY IN THE GLASS

When you get what you want in your struggle for pelf,
And the world makes you king for a day,
Just go to the mirror and look at yourself,
And see what that guy has to say.

For it isn't your father or mother or wife
Who judgment upon you must pass,
The feller whose verdict counts most in your life
Is the one staring back from the glass.

He's the feller to please, never mind all the rest,
For he's with you clear up to the end,
And you've passed your most dangerous, difficult test,
If the guy in the glass is your friend.

You can fool the whole world down the pathway of years,
And get pats on the back as you pass,
But your final reward will be heartaches and tears,
If you've cheated the guy in the glass.

—PETER DALE WIMBROW, SR.

INDISPENSABLE MAN

Sometime when you're feeling important,
Sometime when your ego's in bloom,
Sometime when you take it for granted
You're the best qualified in the room,
Sometime when you feel that your going
Would leave an unfillable hole,
Just follow these simple instructions
And see how they humble your soul:
Take a bucket and fill it with water.
Put your hand in it up to the wrist.
Pull it out, and the hole that's remaining
Is a measure of how you'll be missed.
You can splash all you please when you enter.
You may stir up the water galore.
But stop and you'll find in a minute
That it looks quite the same as before.
The moral to this quaint example
Is do just the best that you can.
Be proud of yourself but remember,
There's no indispensable man.

—SAXON WHITE KESSINGER

IF

If you can keep your head when all about you
Are losing theirs and blaming it on you,
If you can trust yourself when all men doubt you
But make allowance for their doubting too,
If you can wait and not be tired by waiting,
Or being lied about, don't deal in lies,
Or being hated, don't give way to hating,
And yet don't look too good, nor talk too wise:

If you can dream—and not make dreams your master,
If you can think—and not make thoughts your aim;
If you can meet with Triumph and Disaster
And treat those two impostors just the same;
If you can bear to hear the truth you've spoken
Twisted by knaves to make a trap for fools,
Or watch the things you gave your life to, broken,
And stoop and build 'em up with worn-out tools:

If you can make one heap of all your winnings
And risk it all on one turn of pitch-and-toss,
And lose, and start again at your beginnings
And never breathe a word about your loss;
If you can force your heart and nerve and sinew
To serve your turn long after they are gone,
And so hold on when there is nothing in you
Except the Will which says to them: "Hold on!"

If you can talk with crowds and keep your virtue,
Or walk with kings—nor lose the common touch,
If neither foes nor loving friends can hurt you,
If all men count with you, but none too much;

If you can fill the unforgiving minute
With sixty seconds' worth of distance run,
Yours is the Earth and everything that's in it,
And—which is more—you'll be a Man, my son!

—RUDYARD KIPLING

Photo Appendix

Page 2 TOP LEFT: My mom and dad, with me on my 1st birthday
    TOP RIGHT: My mother's favorite baby picture of me
    MIDDLE: My mother, my brothers, and me, Easter 1961
    BOTTOM LEFT: My father, age 3, 1932
    BOTTOM RIGHT: My mother, age 1, 1926

Page 12 TOP LEFT: My Eagle Scout portrait (photo courtesy of
    Buddy Stewart)
    TOP RIGHT: My 1st grade picture, 1961
    MIDDLE: Sharing a moment with some of the Haskell
    Scholars in Amory, Mississippi, 1997 (photo courtesy
    of *People* magazine)
    BOTTOM: On the sidelines of an Amory Panther football
    game with my high school mentor, coach Earl Stevens
    (photo courtesy of Buddy Stewart)

Page 34 TOP: My freshman picture at Ole Miss, 1973
    MIDDLE LEFT: Members of "The Group" during one of
    our concerts at Ole Miss, 1977. I am on the far left,
    Marsha Hull is to my right, and Mary is on the far
    right. (photo courtesy of Buddy Stewart)
    MIDDLE RIGHT: Miss Mississippi knocking her opponent
    into the mud pit
    BOTTOM: Mary and me the morning after she was
    crowned Miss Mississippi, 1977

Page 58 TOP RIGHT: Me and "The Bitch Patrol" Jean Sanders,
    Ellen Boyd, and Dot Forbus (photo courtesy of
    Buddy Stewart)
    TOP LEFT: The 1998 "Stars Over Mississippi" concert
    (photo courtesy of Buddy Stewart)
    MIDDLE RIGHT: My aunt Betty, with HRH the Prince
    Edward in Amory, 1998

MIDDLE LEFT: Jaleel White, Mary, Vince Gill, Nell
     Carter, me, and Debbie Allen, at the 1996 "Stars Over
     Mississippi" concert (photo courtesy of Buddy Stewart)
BOTTOM: Mary, Sam IV, me, our dear friend, Doris
     Roberts, and Mary Lane (photo courtesy of
     Buddy Stewart)

Page 80   TOP TO BOTTOM, FROM LEFT TO RIGHT:
     Me, Whoopi Goldberg, Ally Romano, and Ray Romano
     at the 2002 "Stars Over Mississippi" concert (photo
     courtesy of Buddy Stewart)
     My induction into the Ole Miss Alumni Hall of Fame,
     with Mary, Aunt Betty, Mary Rogers, Marsha and
     Frank Tindall, and Uncle Hal
     Mary and me with my childhood friend, Randy Hollis,
     and his wife, Margie, 1982
     Debbie Allen and me at Debbie's 50th birthday
     Jason Winters, Kathy Ireland, and Erik Sterling with me
     at the 2002 "Stars Over Mississippi" concert (photo
     courtesy of Buddy Stewart)
     Me and Kathie Lee Gifford on my 25th birthday, 1982
     Me and Kirstie Alley (photo courtesy Alex Berliner
     Studios)
     Dolly Parton and me, Christmas 1999
     Me with Jon and Les Moonves at the 21 Club in New
     York, a week after we closed the *Everybody Loves
     Raymond* deal (photo courtesy of Don Pollard)
     Our college friends Nancy White, Marsha and Frank
     Tindall, Louise Burney, Charlie Abraham, and Ben
     Foster at the Miss America Ball in Atlantic City, 1977

Page 102   TOP: The Ray Romano team, including Rory Rosegarten
     and Jon Moonves

MIDDLE LEFT: Sam IV's 2nd birthday party, the day we almost lost *The Fresh Prince of Bel-Air*

MIDDLE RIGHT: Mary and me on our wedding day, December 28, 1982

BOTTOM: Me with newly crowned Miss America 2009, Katie Stam (photo courtesty of Bruce Boyajian)

Page 134 TOP LEFT: Shirley Donnelly, Leslie Wilson, and Sam IV helping me celebrate my 50th birthday in Scotland, 2005

TOP RIGHT: Me with Mary Lane and Sam IV, 1990

MIDDLE LEFT: The Haskell Family, Christmas 2001

MIDDLE RIGHT: Mary and me with Michael Feinstein and Terrence Flannery after Mary Lane's debut at Carnegie Hall, 2007

BOTTOM LEFT: My favorite picture of my girls, Mary and Mary Lane, 2006 (photo courtesy of Mary Ann Halpin Photography)

BOTTOM RIGHT: Mary surprising me on my 40th birthday, 1995

Page 162 TOP: "Lily for President", NBC. I'm in the Richard Nixon mask

MIDDLE: Mary and me with our dear friends, Their Royal Highnesses The Prince and Princess Edward, Earl and Countess of Wessex, 2002 (photo courtesy of Alex Berliner Studios)

BOTTOM: The Haskell Family with our dear friends, Doris Roberts, Debbie Allen, and Kathie Lee Gifford at Glamis Castle in Scotland to celebrate my 50th birthday

Page 174 TOP: The Haskell Family with First Lady Laura Bush after a screening at the White House of Mary's TV

movie, *Twice Upon a Christmas,* co-starring our dear
friend Kathy Ireland

MIDDLE LEFT: With my two mentors, Norman Brokaw
and Jerry Katzman

MIDDLE RIGHT: One of my favorite pictures with three-
year-old Mary Lane at the first press conference for
"Stars Over Mississippi," 1992

BOTTOM: Photo session outside the William Morris of-
fices, 2002 (photo courtesy of Chuck Ross, *TV Week*
magazine)

Page 194   TOP RIGHT: Ole Miss Chancellor Robert Khayat and me,
1998

TOP LEFT: Me, Morgan Freeman, and producer
Michael Seligman preparing for a charity function
at Ole Miss, 2003

MIDDLE: The Cast of "Stars Over Mississippi," 2004
(photo courtesy of Buddy Stewart)

BOTTOM LEFT: Mary and me, "Stars Over Mississippi,"
2000 (photo courtesy of Buddy Stewart)

BOTTOM RIGHT: Mary and me with our friend Sela Ward
(photo courtesy Alex Berliner Studios)

Page 206   TOP: My mother, age 28, 1953

BOTTOM: Mary and me, 2008 (photo courtesy of
Mary Ann Halpin Photography)

*Unless otherwise indicated, photos courtesy of the
Sam and Mary Haskell Collection*

Acknowledgments

I have so many people to thank in terms of helping me make *Promises I Made My Mother* into a reality. Neither my mother nor I could have ever imagined the reach of her lessons. This book now makes it possible. My journey has been blessed with many wonderful friends and family members, many of whom you have met in this book. I wish I could have mentioned every single person in a specific story, but in order to be true to the concept of the book, it just wasn't possible. I can, however, mention many of you here, and that's exactly what I intend to do. For those of you whose names don't appear, I ask your forgiveness. You will always live in my heart.

First, I want to thank my co-author, David Rensin, for his patience and understanding during this process. David has written many bestselling books, and he made it easy for me to open up and share my life. I've always enjoyed writing and telling my stories and anecdotes, but it was David's focus and vision that helped bring them all together—not to mention keeping me on schedule. He's also one of the coolest guys I know!

I am so grateful to Ray Romano for writing the hilarious and touching foreword to this book, and also for just being my pal. My mother would have loved Ray and his wife Anna, and I'm so sorry that she didn't have the chance to know them. Ray makes me laugh, gives great advice, and I want to be just like him when I grow up!

I also have to thank my agents Nancy Josephson and Richard Abate at the Endeavor Agency in Beverly Hills. Nancy had encouraged me to write this book for several years, and after she introduced me to her partner Richard Abate, he convinced me that this would be an experience that I would enjoy. As always, Richard was right! I was thrilled when Random House/Ballantine secured the rights. Publisher Libby McGuire, Executive Editor Susan Mercandetti, Editors Abigail Plesser and Millicent Bennett, Publicity and Marketing Heads Brian McLendon, Carol Schneider, Brant Joneway, Diana Franco, and Lisa Barnes, as well as Tom Perry, Jack Perry, and Rachel Bernstein have been nothing short of wonderful to deal with. They have all made this part of my journey an absolute dream come true.

I must also thank my Mississippi publicists and dear friends Nancy White Perkins and Beth Kellogg. They have mobilized our terrific friends in Mississippi to create book signing events and speaking engagements for me all over the state, and I am most appreciative.

I have known Lisa Kasteler, my national publicist, for almost thirty years. Lisa's honesty, integrity, and relationships have benefited Mary and me greatly. I thank her for her friendship, her life lessons, and her "thoughtful" help in the promotion of this book.

Also, special thanks must go to my assistants Will Cleckler and Kevin Kelly for their support, confidence, and loyalty. Writing a book while running three different charitable foundations has been an arduous task, but Will and Kevin helped keep me focused and on deadline, and for that I will be eternally grateful.

Jeff Goldberg was my last assistant at William Morris and my first assistant as Mary and I began our next chapter in the world of philanthropy and the promotion of Mary's music career. Jeff was also one of my assistants during the production of *Mississippi Rising* for MSNBC, and we thank him for his continued loyalty and support.

After thirty years, Don DeMesquita knows me as well as anyone in my life, and it was he who came up with the title for this book. I thank him most humbly for his constant belief in me and in my dreams.

I would like to thank The Miss America Organization Board of Directors for their support of me these past four years. They are: Rebecca King Dreman, Ryan Wuerch, Donna Axum Whitworth, John Bermingham, Phyllis George, Lynn Weidner, Ron Burkhardt, Paul Turcotte, Tammy Haddad, Ed Peterson, Corinne Sparenberg, and Barrie Jane Tracy. I must also mention and thank the incredible people who make up the Miss America Organization Staff—President and CEO Art McMaster, Rick Brinkley, Sharon Pearce, Mike Allegretto, Kirk Ryder, Pat Gianni, Joann Silver, Liz Puro, Lauren O'Donnell, Bonnie Mac Isaac, Doreen Gordon, and Mary Ellen Lucia. John Ferriter, our wonderful agent at William Morris, has been a stalwart ally to me in our search to ultimately find a terrific television partnership with TLC/Discovery—he will never know how much I appreciate his loyalty, his class, and his friendship. My appreciation must also be shared with Robert Earl, Tom McCartney, and Bill Feather at Planet Hollywood, and with TLC's Eileen O'Neill, Nancy Daniels, Brent Zacky, Selma Edelman, Edward Sabin, Angela Shapiro-Mathes, and Angela Molloy. Many of the Miss America Organization State Executive Directors were among the first to stand by my side as I introduced a new vision for the pageant. I will forever appreciate their support and loyalty. They are a family of volunteers acting as one, and I appreciate each of them more than they know.

My years at Ole Miss were some of the happiest years of my life. I made many lifelong friends, and I cherish them all. In addition, my sincere appreciation must be shared with Ole Miss Chancellor Robert Khayat and his wife Margaret, Ole Miss Vice Chancellor Gloria Kellum and her husband Jerry, and countless other faculty and alumni friends including Barry and Angelyn Cannada, Mary Ann and Don Frugé, Patty and Will Lewis, Jan and Lawrence Farrington, Helen and Cooper Thurber, Joy and Bill Aden, Joy and Frank Tindall, Sr., Pat and Briggs Hopson, Linda Spargo, Matt and Rhonda Lusco, Cynthia Linton, Rose Flenorl, Dr. Dan Jones, Diane and Dick Scruggs, and my longtime friend David Brevard. I served with many of these friends while working on several University-based philanthropic projects on the Oxford campus and beyond: Producing a *Celebration of Mississippi Leadership Honoring Trent Lott*, Co-chairing the Ole Miss Momentum Capital Campaign, and Co-chairing the Advisory Board of the Gertrude C. Ford Center for the Performing Arts with my friend Morgan Freeman. And finally, I must thank the gracious people of Oxford, Mississippi, our new home, who will now be a part of our hearts forever.

My thanks must also be extended to my special friend Debbie Allen, Norman Nixon, and my fellow Board Members of the Debbie Allen Dance Academy, and to the Television Academy of Arts and Sciences Chairman Dick Askin for appointing me Chairman of the TV Academy Hall of Fame Selection Committee. Thanks also to The Duke Of Edinburgh's Award Young Americans' Challenge Board members John Danielson, Lanny Griffith, Manley Thaler, and Linda Amara as well as all of our founding patrons for supporting my dream of bringing this wonderful International Award Program to the United States. Created by HRH The Duke of Edinburgh and executed today by my good friend HRH The Prince Edward, we have already expanded The Award into fourteen states!

I am so proud of the incredible people of Amory, Mississippi, who nurtured me during my youth and, as an adult, supported my dream of raising over four million dollars for the Mary Kirkpatrick Haskell Scholarship Foundation. Thanks must go to the Foundation Governing Board: Dot Forbus, Ellen Boyd, Jean Sanders, Dan Rogers, Steve and Cynthia Greenhaw, Steve and Darlene Stockton, and Dianne Young; and Stars Over Mississippi Concert Chairmen: Jean Pinkley and Carolyn Koenig, who all helped mobilize hundreds of volunteers in Amory to execute our Stars Over Mississippi concerts. I wish I could name them all, but additional thanks must go to volunteers Peggy Holmes, Missy Gary, Dan Sanders, Judy Dobbs, Doug and Stephanie Fowlkes, the McGonagill family, the Hollis family, the Mississippi National Guard, and the incomparable Judy Holman. Performers from all over the country came to Amory and touched many lives, so my thanks, herein, must also go to each of the "Stars Over Mississippi" who performed in Amory during seven incredible concerts. They include: Kathie Lee Gifford, Sandi Patti, Wil Shriner, Mary Haskell, Guy Hovis, Gary Grubbs, Mary Ann Mobley, Gary Collins, Dean Butler, Debbie Allen, Collin Ray, Malcolm Jamal Warner, Nell Carter, Susan Anton, Lynn Randle, Dawn Keenum, Kathy Ireland, Sela Ward, The Gents, Vince Gill, Joan van Ark, Jaleel White, Donna Axum, Phil Hartman, HRH The Prince Edward, Bryan White, Pam Tillis, Marilyn McCoo & Billy Davis, Jr., Laurie Gayle Stephenson, Ashley Buckman, Jalin Wood, Jennifer Adcock, Diahann Carroll, Christy May, John Dye, Tom Arnold, Marilu Henner, Ann-Margret, Dolly Parton, Brooke Shields, Marsha Tindall, Brooks & Dunn, Ray Romano, Whoopi Goldberg, Delta Burke, Gerald McRaney, Wynonna Judd, Brad Paisley, Brad Garrett, Doris Roberts, Michael Feinstein, Kirstie Alley, Lance Bass, Tony Danza, Patricia Heaton, David Hunt, Jean Smart, Sean Hayes, U.S. Secretary of Education Dr. Rod Paige, U.S. Senator Trent

Lott, U.S. Senator Roger Wicker, Governor Ronnie Musgrove, and Governor and Mrs. Haley Barbour. I will forever be grateful to Ray Caldiero and Cindy Wozniak at Northwest Airlines, as well as Rick Shipp, Paul Moore, Greg Oswald, and Rob Beckham, my William Morris associates in Nashville, for their help in graciously delivering so many of my concert headliners.

The success of my philanthropic efforts depends on the support of the media. In Hollywood, I could not have been more fortunate to have had the support of Elizabeth Guider at the *Hollywood Reporter,* Cynthia Littleton at *Daily Variety,* Chuck Ross at *TV Week,* and Scott Collins at the *Los Angeles Times.* In Mississippi, Chris Wilson at the Monroe *County Journal,* Scott Morris and Billy Crews at the Tupelo *Daily Journal,* Marilyn Smith of Metro Christian Living, and Ronnie Agnew at the Jackson *Clarion Ledger* are all special friends, whose support has meant the world to me.

We all need people to look up to and to emulate. I'd like to thank my Hollywood mentors: William Morris' Norman Brokaw, Larry Auerbach, Hal Ross, Jerry Katzman, Walter Zifkin, Richard Rosenberg, Steve Kram, Lou Weiss, and Tony Fantozzi; Emmy-winning producer George Schlatter; network legend Fred Silverman; CAA's Lee Gabler; CBS' Leslie Moonves; and NBC's Brandon Tartikoff. I learned from their example that encouraged me to serve as a mentor to my many co-workers at William Morris and beyond. Those trainees/assistants who helped keep me focused and on task include Maria Carillo, Sally Nussbaum, Greg Lipstone, Tracy Kramer, Neil Bagg, Rob Carlson, George Stelzner, Alan Greenspan, Scott Howard, David Kopoloff, Mike Mayne, Alex Chaice, Jeff Kolodny, Curt Northrop, Rob Wolken, Jack Leighton, Kevin Litt, Jason Trawick, Kirk Ryder, Gordon Kaywin, Andrew Salute, Ryan Wooten, Jeff Goldberg, Patton Valentine, Jason Morey, and Stephen Kirkpatrick. There are those we grow up with (or grow older with) who also have a great im-

pact on our business and personal lives, so I'd also like to thank
Mark Itkin, Cara Stein, Cori Wellins, Lanny Noveck, Mike
Simpson, Cary Berman, Biff Liff, Peter Grosslight, Pat Galloway,
Christopher Walsh, Marilyn Bloom, Erik Seastrand, Rob Carl-
son, Jim Griffin, David Lonner, Alan Gasmer, Jim Ornstein, Jon
Rosen, David Kekst, Robyn Goldman, Susan Brooks, Ruth En-
glehardt, Suzy Unger, Scott Henderson, Holly Baril, Michael
Cooper, Jeff Robin, Peter Franklin, Stuart Christenfeld, Michael
Dates, Brian Rabolli, Steve Weiss, Collin Reno, Randi Michel,
John Mass, Stu Tenzer, Ann Blanchard, Dick Alen, Rene Kurtz,
John Ferriter, and Irv Weintraub at William Morris; Nancy Tel-
lum and Nina Tassler at CBS; Jeff Zucker, Dick Ebersol, Ben Sil-
verman and Marc Graboff at NBC; Mark Pedowitz, Steve
McPherson, Anne Sweeney, Laurie Younger, and Bob Iger at
ABC/Disney; Gail Berman at Berman/Braun Productions; Peter
Chernin, Kevin Reilly, Hutch Parker, Tony Sella (and Peggy) and
Mike Darnell at 20th Century Fox; Robert Greenblatt, Beth
Klein, and Jerry Offsay at Showtime; ICM's Greg Lipstone and
Bob Broder; CAA's Bryan Lourd, Kevin Huvane, and Steve Laf-
ferty; Paradigm's Sam Gores and Bill Douglass; agents Steve
Glick, Bruce Brown, and Bradford Bricken; Dawn Ostroff at the
CW; Wal-Mart's Lee and Linda Scott, Viking's Fred Carl and
Dale Persons; BancorpSouth's Aubrey Patterson, Randy Burch-
field and Pam Armour; Steve Mosko at Sony; Bruce Rosenblum
and Peter Roth at Warner Bros.; Jeffrey Katzenberg at Dream-
Works; and Cliff and Leslie Gilbert-Lurie at the Alliance for
Children's Rights; Gary Newman and Dana Walden at Twenti-
eth Century Fox Television; NAB's Eddie Fritts (and Martha
Dale); Universal Music's Paul Cooper; Jon Feltheimer and Kevin
Beggs at Lionsgate; Harry Sloan at MGM; Chef Robert St. John;
Artist Bill Dunlap; Artist Jason Bouldin (and Alicia); Artist Gail
Pittman, Musical Director Steven Cahill; Martingale Music's
Eric Wyse; producer Larry Gordon; producer Allen Sviridoff;

producer Pat Tourk Lee; manager Garry Kief; manager Andy Murcia; producer Billy Campbell; producer Terry Botwick (and Moncita); producer Bud Schaetzle; director Ted Sprague; art director James Gray; producers Pamela K. Long and Steven Brackley; producer Tom Leonardis; HBO's Bob Crestani; producers Gary and Rita Considine; producer Michael Filerman; producer Gil Cates; Governor Arnold Schwarzenegger and First Lady Maria Shriver; KCET's Mare Mazur; Sherry Lansing and David Stapf at Paramount; producer Don Mischer; manager Deborah Miller; my awesome Miss America telecast producers Tony Eaton and Lauren Harris; writer Lewis Friedman; Viewpoint School's Kris Dworkoski, Laurel Tew, Doris Warren, Lisa Kakassy, Chris Rosko, Paul Rosenbaum, and Headmaster Robert Dworkoski; New Roads School's Pat McCabe (and Nancy), and Headmaster David Bryan; Lifetime's Andrea Wong, Carole Black and Joann Alfono; Tribune's Dick Askin and Ed Wilson; art director Rene Lagler; Morey Management's Jim and Jason Morey; director Stephen Sommers; producer Andrew Solt, producer Rory Rosegarten; attorney Laurel Kaufer, Tijuana Productions' John Foy, Troy Searer, and Wally Parks; manager Darla Blake, manager Andy Howard; producer Kerry McCluggage, manager Bernie Brillstein; manager Barry Krost, producer Michael Seligman; producer Brenda Hampton; producers Ron Cowen and Daniel Lipman; director David Trainer (and Deborah); Paley Center's Barbara Dixon; manager Phyllis Rab Elkins; Stevie's Restaurant owners—Stevie and Leslie Perry; Wolfgang Puck and all the gang at Spago; Greg Pappas at the Bistro Garden; Colleen, Rob, Stephanie, Freddie, Angela, Jessica, and everyone at Jerry's Deli in Encino—my second office; and special artists like Ann Jillian, Martin Short, Betty White, Virginia Williams, Kim Coles, Allison Kellogg, Chris Matthews, Nita Whitaker, Brad Maule, Ryan Seacrest, Marie Osmond, Regis Philbin, Michael Young, Sam Harris, Michele Lee, Laura Bell Bundy, Kate Shindle,

Donna Mills, Mary Hart, Lynda Carter, Jenifer Lewis, Susan Sullivan, Ann Rutherford, G. W. Bailey, Swoosie Kurtz, Gretchen Carlson, Susan Powell, Kirsten Haglund, Katie Stam, Don Johnson, Julie Chen, Barry Manilow, Jill Conner Browne, Diane Ladd, Rick and Julie Dees, Liza Minnelli, Phylicia Rashad, Vanessa Williams, Red Buttons, and Morgan Freeman.

I must add recognition for the Sam and Mary support team: attorneys Mitch Whitehead, Donna Melby, Ernie Del, Jon Moonves, John Creekmore, and Sam Griffie; CPA Danny Howard; Investment Manager Graham O'Kelly; Doctors Steve Rabin, Charles Kivowitz, Bill Dorfman, Bill Bauer, Laurence Neuman, and Joe Sugarman, Bank of America's Joanne Steenson; Zegna's Noah Alexander; Travel agents David Odaka and Terri Lim; Dean Butler at Legacy Entertainment; Quinn Monahan at Q&A Productions; and our trusted housekeepers Ana Lemus and Marjorie (Sonja) Bennett. Each of you enriches our lives in more ways than you'll ever know, and we love you!

Their Royal Highnesses The Prince And Princess Edward Earl and Countess of Wessex, AKA Edward and Sophie Wessex, and their children Louise and James, have been a blessing in our lives for almost thirteen years. I discussed the special relationship we share in this book, but I also want to mention our dear mutual friend Jeanye "Tex" Irwin, and the entire Wessex staff and PPOs. I appreciate what each of you mean to their Royal Highnesses, but I especially appreciate your many kindnesses to me and my family.

Shirley and Bob Donnelly, Mary's parents, have been the most awesome in-laws I could have ever wished for. From the moment Mary and I started dating, Bob and Shirley welcomed me into their incredible family, and I love them dearly. We lost Bob several years ago, but Shirley has continued on as the matriarch of Mary's family. She is one classy lady, and someone whose respect I truly treasure. Mary's sisters Pride and Leslie have become my sisters as well. Along with their husbands, Richard Parr and Bill Wilson, and our nieces and nephews, they make our family complete.

Marsha and Frank Tindall have played important roles in our lives since we first met at Ole Miss. They flew to Atlantic City to be with me and our families when Mary competed at Miss America, they were both attendants in our wedding party, and they were in California for the births of our children. Frank is even the architectual designer of our new home in Oxford. Our journeys and our families have been intertwined for thirty-five years. The very thought of Marsha and Frank always makes me smile, and I thank them both for their constant support and special love.

My father's sister Marilyn and her husband Dr. Bill Graf have been two of the most supportive and loving influences in my life. Aunt Marilyn and Uncle Bill have made me proud of my Haskell roots, and they've helped me understand my father. My first cousins Christy, Bill, Jr., Josie, and Amy, are all incredibly lovely people, and I've always been so proud of each and every one of them.

My brothers Jamie and Billy know that I love them, and I hope that they will always remember how much their mother loved them too!

Susie, Bill and Blake Ewing are truly our extended family in Los Angeles. The Ewing/Haskell "family tour," especially during the Christmas holidays, is one of the things I look forward to most. . . . including special "pig-outs" on Susie's Texas caviar, and our trips to Disneyland. Thank you Ewings, for loving us unconditionally!

Our dear Mississippi friends Glenda and Gary Grubbs and their children Molly and Logan will always hold a very special place in our hearts. Glenda was also a Miss Mississippi and Gary was the best man in our wedding. They were two of the very first friends we made in Los Angeles, and we love them so much!

You may have noticed that there is a recurring theme in my

life when it comes to Miss Mississippi! So I would be remiss if I didn't acknowledge three of my all-time favorites. Mary Ann Mobley, Miss Mississippi and Miss America 1959, Lynda Mead Shea, Miss Mississippi and Miss America 1960, and Chalie Carroll Ray, Miss Mississippi 1962, are all such remarkably talented women, and the laughter and friendship we have shared through the years has brought Mary, the children, and me such joy.

Pam Long and Steve Brackley have been a source of support, humor, and inspiration to me and my family for many years, as have Pastor Carolyn "Care" Crawford and her husband Steve Madaris, and Todd and Laurie Stephenson Caliguire. I hope that I've made them as happy as they have made me.

Eric Schotz is a very talented producer, but he is an extraordinary friend. I cherish his advice. During my days at William Morris, and after my resignation, there has never been a single week that has passed in which Eric hasn't called to check on me. I'll always appreciate him for that, and for a friendship we should all be so lucky to have.

What a blessing it was when Michael Feinstein and Terrence Flannery came into our lives. Mary and I have loved Michael's music for decades! I really do believe that people come into our lives for a reason—to share joy, to learn lessons, or to make a difference—our friendship with Michael and Terrence has meant all of that and more.

Wil Shriner and Hudson Hickman were two of my "first" best friends in Hollywood. Wil, a talented comedian and director, hails from Indiana, and Hudson, a prolific television producer, hails from my home state of Mississippi. We stood up for each other in each of our weddings, our children have grown up together, and to this day we mourn the loss of our dear friend Mike Wagner, who was part of our original "Four Amigos" group who hung out at the Gardens of Taxco Mexican Restaurant every Friday night in the early '80s.

Erik Sterling, Jason Winters, Jon Carrasco, and Stephen Roseberry have been a part of our lives for over twenty years. Their love, loyalty, counsel, devoted friendship, and understanding of all things make them the "best of the best." Sam IV and Mary Lane have four wonderful godfathers and Mary and I have four incredible brothers.

Betty and Hal Rogers are my surrogate parents now, and I hope that I've made them proud. They will never know what it means to me that they are Sam and Mary Lane's Mississippi grandparents. My mother loved and respected them so much and so do I!

My cousins Mary, Dan, Carol and Katie Rogers, Mary Nan Kirkpatrick Hodo, James Richard Kirkpatrick, Sammie and Hubert Elliott, and Nan Elliott Moon will never know how much I appreciate their love and support. As I look back on my life, my Rogers/Kirkpatrick/Elliott cousins were there every step of the way. You guys are priceless, and I love you with all of my heart—my mother did too!

Sam IV and Mary Lane entered our world in 1988 and 1989, respectively. The children were born 16 months apart, so for them and for us, it has been like raising twins. Neither of them knows a time when the other wasn't there. I love them both so much. They are the joy of my life. Sam is an incredibly intelligent and handsome young man. His dreams are our dreams, and Mary and I have always felt that God has a special destiny in store for Sam. Watching him excel at football and volleyball in Middle School, and then seeing him master his martial arts training in high school, earning his Black Belt, shows his dedication to a task and his character. At age 21, Sam is studying Film production at California State University in Northridge and I can't wait to see his life unfold. Mary Lane has had a special presence since she was a toddler. Her joyful spirit is contagious. Mary Lane's dedication to her life in the performing arts, whether with her high school mentor, Director Dorris Warren, or now in college, allows her to shine brightly through her work on stage. Watching Mary Lane perform has always been pure joy for me. She shows a maturity on stage that is almost undefinable, and I know that she has a brilliant future ahead of her. Her studies continue at NYU in the prestigious CAP 21 Musical Theatre BFA program under the leadership of Frank and Eliza Ventura through The Tisch School of the Arts.

What can I say about Mary Donnelly Haskell, except that she is a dream come true. It's a fact that as a little boy, I told my mother that I would marry a Miss Mississippi one day. But Mary is so much more. Yes, she is stunningly beautiful, yes, she is extremely talented, yes, she's a wonderful mother, wife, and friend, and yes, she has a servant's heart. But what makes Mary so incredibly special is that she knows "how" to guide everyone she comes in contact with to be their personal best. Some might call her inspirational. . . . I call her magical. She knows me so well, and her unconditional support and loyalty mean everything to me. God certainly knew what he was doing when he brought us together. There is no better mate for me in this world than Mary. I love her for lots of reasons, but I love her most because I know without a doubt that she loves me!

— SAM HASKELL

———

When I interviewed Sam Haskell in 2002 for *The Mailroom*, my oral history of starting at the bottom in show business, dreaming of the top, I knew immediately that he stood out from the usual Hollywood crowd. He was tall, from Mississippi, drew widespread praise for his attitudes and ethics, and behaved without artifice based on deeply felt values that, he explained, he'd been taught by his mother. This is not something you often hear in the ambition factories of Beverly Hills. Five years later, when Sam asked me to help him write this book, I quickly said yes, even temporarily putting aside a project I'd already begun. I'm glad I did. The experience, our friendship, and the result you're reading surpasses rewarding. Thanks, Sam.

I'd also like to thank Sara Rimensnyder, who transcribed all the tapes, shared her wise analyses, and then helped me find my way through to the end.

And thanks to everyone at Random House/Ballantine, for making it easy.

My enduring love and affection for my wife, Suzie Peterson, and son, Emmett Rensin, who unselfishly share me with my work. And, of course: Mom—this is for you.

— DAVID RENSIN

ABOUT THE AUTHORS

SAM HASKELL moved from Mississippi to Los Angeles in 1978 to work at the William Morris Agency. He became an agent in 1980, senior vice president by 1990, executive vice president by 1995, and Worldwide Head of Television by 1999. After a twenty-six-year career, he retired in 2004 to pursue philanthropic endeavors. In 2007 he was named one of the 25 Most Innovative and Influential People in Television over the last quarter century by *TV Week*. He lives in Los Angeles with his wife, Mary Donnelly Haskell (his college sweetheart and a former Miss Mississippi), and their two children, Sam IV and Mary Lane.

www.promisesimademymother.com

DAVID RENSIN has written or co-written thirteen books, five of them *New York Times* bestsellers. His most recent titles are *All for a Few Perfect Waves: The Audacious Life and Legend of Rebel Surfer Miki Dora* and *The Mailroom: Hollywood History from the Bottom Up*.

ABOUT THE TYPE

This book was set in Fairfield, the first typeface from the hand of the distinguished American artist and engraver Rudolph Ruzicka (1883–1978). Ruzicka was born in Bohemia and came to America in 1894. He set up his own shop, devoted to wood engraving and printing, in New York in 1913 after a varied career working as a wood engraver, in photoengraving and banknote printing plants, and as an art director and freelance artist. He designed and illustrated many books, and was the creator of a considerable list of individual prints—wood engravings, line engravings on copper, and aquatints.